AF316798

Love's Labor Lost:

Ten Mothers Share their Journey from Grief to Hope

Transcribed and written by
Ruth Ellen Johnson

Cover art by
Lidice Cohen

_To Cindy, Diana, Leigh Ann, Jami, Perla, Marci,
Suzy, Susan, Judy, Angie…_

_Gratitude for the willingness to share your fractured
hearts._
_May your brave transparency be rewarded tenfold and
spurn others to help and hope._

Table of Contents

Prologue

"This is not the way it's supposed to be. Parents aren't supposed to bury their children."

You've heard it over and over. Too many times, perhaps. But is it true? When was that statute given?

Sadly, it wasn't. It is a heartfelt sentiment, a sense of God's perfection residing in us. But it isn't scriptural or historical. A fallen world is a truth in which we live—a world where there is death and tragedy recorded for us from the earliest stages of mankind. Adam and Eve had to bury Abel.

We, in the 21st century, live in the age of formidable healthcare where children usually do outlive their parents. But barely 200 years ago, parents lost many children in childbirth or childhood disease. Only 46% lived to adulthood. Did they handle it better because it was so common? Possibly. But I don't believe in any era that losing a child was easy. A mother's love from the moment of conception to love's labor lost is a crushing blow.

I almost lost a child. She was 3 yrs. old when her appendix leaked, turned gangrene, and filled her with poison. After three back-to-back surgeries, we were told doctors would keep doing surgeries till the poison was gone or she died from so many procedures. And an extremely high percentage of children her age died. One dark night in the hospital, I sat alone, watching her tiny little body fight for life. They had decided to leave the surgical cut open all the way down her thoracic cavity for easier access as they knew more surgeries were likely. She looked wretched and bloody, with tubes and monitors everywhere. I cried out to the Lord with everything in me, beseeching him to save her. And in a still, small voice, He answered. He asked if I could give her back to him. "What?!! No! No, no, no, Lord! I love her! Her birth was so difficult; she was in my womb almost 11 months. She was born on Christmas Day, Lord!"

And yet again, He gently spoke, "Could you entrust her to me and believe I know what is best and that I love her more than you do?"

Even in my fledgling faith, I knew it was true. And despite my wailing...I submitted. I lifted my arms and returned her to Him.

The next morning, she was markedly improved and continued to skyrocket back to health. He had healed her and restored her back to us. And she has been a blessing and delight her entire toe-shoed life. She has a lingering after-effect that puts us on guard every few years—emergency room runs to clear a blockage. It's a sober reminder of the privilege we've had and the precious years we've been given.

The mothers within these pages did not receive my answer. They had to face their wanting arms and splintered hearts. Their journeys in these chapters are honest and transparent, and sometimes raw. This is the way it was for them. Grief has etched their souls. It is not about their dead—they are gone. It is about them, the ones left behind, living with the echo.

These moms are not seeking Pulitzers; they are seeking peace. And they are hoping to render grace to other mothers caught in the chasm of tear-soaked pillows, empty shoes, and silence where a voice once called, "Mom". These brave souls are moving on to find joy from ashes, hoping to shoulder others along with them. Handle them with care; no grief is the same. There is no set process, no set formula.

These saints are my heroes, and I have been blessed and privileged to share in their journeys.

—Ruth Ellen Johnson

Cindy

Mother. Driver. Survivor. Griever. Encourager.

I described my grief experience in five simple words, but there has been nothing simple about my loss.

My grief journey started on Sunday, June 3, 2007. I woke early and excited to fly from our home in Southern California to Northern California, where our youngest daughter Amy met me at the San José airport. Amy and her husband Tyson were moving to Southern California to get their MBAs from UCLA. They would live closer to us and to our other daughter Kelly, her husband, Ryan, and their young children.

Amy picked me up in a van filled with her things. Tyson had one more week of work left before driving down. My husband Jon and I dreamt of our daughters living near each other and to us and raising their children together. It seemed like all the pieces were coming together.

Amy and I laughed and chatted about anything and everything for several hours before stopping to pick up a quick lunch. I offered to drive.

"You know what happens when I get in the passenger seat," Amy said.

"Of course I do, honey. I've known you your whole life. Have a good nap," I said.

"But Mommio, I'm loving this time with you," she said while reclining her seat.

"That's ok, honey. We have all the time in the world."

We were outside Bakersfield, three hours from home when the

car began shimmying. Startled awake, Amy asked what was wrong.

"I don't know, Am," I said. "I'm changing lanes to see if it's the freeway or if we have a prob…"

I never finished the word.

The back left tire exploded, catapulting our van through a fence—hurling us like a spinning top across a large field. The steering wheel spun wildly. I couldn't stop the terror, stop the screaming, stop the horror.

We were a hurtling mass as we rolled repeatedly. Once. Twice. Three times. The white van was an angry monster. I knew our situation was bad and tried to negotiate with God.

"Take me, not Amy. Just not Amy," I prayed.

I felt a momentary calm that didn't fit the situation and sensed God say, "It's not up to you. Trust Me."

Somehow, during the chaos, I managed to say, "I love you, Amo."

I heard her say, "Jesus."

Then nothing.

There was no sound other than my frightened breathing echoing through my aching head. Then a song started in my mind as if on the radio. It was the hymn, "It Is Well with My Soul," which I knew from church. I knew from the history of that particular hymn Amy had not survived.

I was seat-belted in our crumpled van, battered, and surrounded by broken glass.

I cried out, "Oh Amo! I'm so sorry, I'm so sorry…"

I was sure I heard Amy's voice say, "Don't say that, Mommio. Don't worry about me, take care of all of you. It's beautiful...it's so beautiful." I heard her as if she was right beside me.

When our tire exploded, I wasn't speeding or distracted. I hadn't caused the accident, but I was the mother who couldn't stop the world to save her child.

I could hardly move but knew Amy was not in the van. I called out, but there was no response. I slipped in and out of consciousness. Hands maneuvered me out of the wreckage and onto a gurney. I tried looking around. We were in a big field, but I couldn't see Amy. Then I was in an ambulance with a loud siren. The paramedics kept asking questions about me. I kept asking about Amy.

Doors opened and closed, and I was wheeled into a bright emergency room. I asked about Amy.

"You'll have to ask the doctor," replied a young man with big blue eyes.

The doctor was kind and attentive. He said I had only minimal abrasions and didn't need surgery. Nurses said I'd been in an alfalfa field, and they removed most of the alfalfa pieces embedded in my head and arms. I lost a layer of the scalp on the back of my head. I would bruise, but basically, I was fine. At least physically.

A highway patrolman asked me question after question. I gave answer after answer. Still, nobody had answers for me about Amy. I drifted in and out.

Sometime later, the doctor's phone rang. He spoke quietly before gently offering me the phone.

"Jon?" I said.

"I need to tell you about Amy," Jon's voice was hollow, like the insides were carved out. "Cindy, are you there? Can you hear me?" Jon said louder.

"I'm here," I said, sounding like I swallowed cotton.

"She's gone," Jon said. "Amy didn't make it."

The words burned in the air, coating the room with ash. Jon was weeping. I was weeping. Nurses dabbed their eyes. I wanted to throw the phone, to shatter something to keep my life from shattering.

"Cindy, Amy didn't make it," Jon repeated.

God had communicated that message when "It is Well with My Soul" started playing in my mind, but I tried to ignore it. I knew William Spafford wrote that song when the ship he was on was over the spot where his daughters had drowned. God gave me the hymn to tell me I alone survived. In lucid moments, I knew He was sparing me false hope. In motherly moments, I grasped for hope with every ounce of my being. I used to like that hymn. Now I hated it. It was not well with my soul.

I knew Amy didn't make it but hadn't accepted it. I had clutched a sliver of hope since no human voice had uttered those words.

A nurse moved me to a small room. It seemed like forever until Jon and the others arrived. Jon came in first. He was walking in sorrow. We struggled to know what to say. The silence of pain echoed so loudly that there was no space for anything. He told me what it was like having to tell Tyson over the phone. I couldn't imagine.

Jon's parents crept into the room, sad shadows offering hugs and tears. We didn't say much because nothing would bring Amy back. After Jon and his parents left, Kelly came. When she rounded the corner, we melted into each other and into tears.

"Oh, Mom, I am so sorry. I can't believe Amy is gone," she
said, voice breaking. "I'm so thankful you're ok. When we
got the call, nobody knew about you. I don't know what I'd
do if you didn't survive."

I worried about her. She gave birth to James less than three
weeks prior. She left home more than five hours before. She had
to be physically and emotionally empty. Kelly and Amy had
always had a magical sister connection people commented on
frequently.

After Kelly left, friends Phyllis and Teri appeared. They told me
nobody knew what to expect when they saw me. I didn't know
what to expect either. I kept hoping I wasn't me anymore.

Sometime after they left, Tyson came into the room. Agony
radiated from him, yet he gave me a hug.

"Oh, Tyson…" is all I managed to say at first. "Amy…"

"I'm so glad you're okay, Cindy," he said.

I was released from the hospital as night drifted into the
morning. Jon and I drove in silence to our nearby hotel. We
weren't ourselves. It wasn't our life. Jon went to bed. I stared in
the mirror but didn't recognize the haggard woman looking
back. I was dazed, still covered with dirt and alfalfa, hair matted
with blood. I stood on trembling legs in a sizzling shower until I
couldn't stand anymore. I wanted the water to wash away the
last half of Sunday. I hurt everywhere. I climbed into a cold bed.
Jon was acres away on his side. I tossed through the last hours
of the night, trying to make sense of a senseless situation.

On the first slice of the morning, I found Jon's phone and called
my parents. They cried with me. Conversations during breakfast
in the lobby were strained. After much talk, it was time to go.
The drive seemed endless. Jon and I barely spoke.

Before we left Bakersfield, we were told Amy's body would remain for the coroner to perform an autopsy. I couldn't imagine it. Would not. No.

Coming home was hard. Breathing was hard. Life seemed unbearable.

The accident occurred on Sunday afternoon. We arrived home Monday afternoon, and Amy's funeral was on Saturday. In the few days in between, countless people showed up, held us up, and helped us do what needed to be done. We agonized over whether or not to view Amy's body, but after hearing the man at the mortuary suggest we didn't, we chose not to see her in a lifeless, injured state. We knew she was already alive in heaven. We suffered through discussions, deciding to have her cremated and where to place her ashes. Fortunately, we found the right spot at a cemetery near our house.

Our family was on prayer chains and meal trains. It took God's help and many hands to put together Amy's Celebration of Life service. Over 1800 people came. God guided Tyson, Kelly, Ryan, Jon, me, and certain friends to speak. It was beyond painful and sad while still being beyond beautiful and uplifting.

Two days after her memorial, we held a graveside service at the mortuary. It also was beyond painful and sad. However, it wasn't as beautiful and uplifting because I kept staring at the urn filled with Amy's ashes. Just eight days after I'd driven with our bubbly dimpled, strawberry blond, I was staring at an urn of all that remained of her. After the service, Tyson pulled away and stood alone, staring at the urn. I went over and hugged him and opened my mouth, praying for the right words. God came through.

> "Tyson, there is space for you here at the cemetery; you will always be family," I said. "But you belong with your next wife, and I will dance with you at your wedding."

Jon and I did well during Amy's services, but we didn't otherwise. We may have lost the same daughter, but we were worlds different in how we grieved her. We were both living our worst nightmares but had trouble acknowledging the other's anguish. Instead of focusing on shared sorrow, we magnified hurts. The more we noticed our differences, the more there were to notice.

Fortunately, a friend who was a counselor convinced us to come to see him. We went weekly for many months. I also needed individual counseling and went weekly for many months. Amy's death shattered our lives, and it took a long time to recover the pieces and far longer to find new ways to put them together. Thanks to our counseling and much prayer, Jon and I started to connect better. We had a lot to learn and change, accept, and forgive. We admitted we'd pulled away from each other and were lonely because we were going through our tragedy alone – multiplying the tragedy. Our counselor asked us to try to move toward each other, and we slowly built a bridge back to each other.

Something else that helped tremendously was attending a grief support group called *GriefShare*. We learned we had to do the work of grief, that working through our sadness and loss was active, not passive. The passing of time wouldn't heal us. Going to *GriefShare* gave us shared language and experiences. Those weekly evenings held some of the most honest conversations we had since the accident. We grew closer. By going each week, we learned how to live in our new reality. Some of our disconnects melted away as we grew comfortable talking about our pain. We felt safer sharing our emotions. Less defensive.

We kept up our relationship with Tyson. I would have understood him pulling away, but he managed to see beyond his pain and asked about us. We shared Amy-stories and laughed together. We cried together, too, frequently and unapologetically. We knew and loved Tyson as our son-in-law but came to know and love him at a depth carved by shared trauma. Jon, Tyson, and I worked and wept together as we unloaded the container of all of Amy and Tyson's belongings when they arrived. Jon and I listened to Tyson's heart and thoughts about his future without Amy. We helped him move into an apartment as a single man, having previously lived in a home as a happily married one.

We made our way through our first Thanksgiving and Christmas. We tried focusing more on gratitude for all the years we had Amy instead of life ahead without her. We leaned on God and felt He held us up. I journaled my experiences from the very beginning and found my rambling on paper helped untangle my emotions and sometimes brought insight.

"God, I am so broken," I wrote one afternoon before Christmas. I couldn't write anything more. I closed my journal, closed my eyes, and lay down.

"There's more room for me in broken people," I heard God say after a few minutes.

It wasn't an audible voice, I'm not sure how I heard it, but I did—clearly. It was soothing. My body warmed. I almost slid down to kneel but didn't want to risk ending the experience. I didn't need to do anything. I simply had to be. To be broken me. To be loved and comforted by God.

On New Year's Day, I wrote in my journal again. I had survived. Jon and I had survived. Jon and I were more united. Nevertheless, the thought of a new year without Amy felt unbearable.

I journaled: "God, I felt broken before Christmas, but now I feel even more broken. I didn't know that was possible."

In a similar gentle way, I felt God answer: "I shine brighter through brokenness."

I was drawn to others in grief and started inviting others to *GriefShare*. The program was so pivotal in our healing that I wanted others to have the help and hope we did. Today Jon and I lead *GriefShare* at our church, and I am hoping to launch a website, www.surprisedbygrief.com, in 2023.

I never used the word "bittersweet" as much as I did during those early months after Amy died. I couldn't believe how bitter life felt and tasted, but I also couldn't believe how sweet God had been. I felt His comfort and presence in ways I never had before, but I had never been as desperate for Him before. When I woke during the night, I felt like He scooped me up and wrapped His arms around me until I fell back asleep.

Focusing on gratitude helped, and I had much to be grateful for. Jon and I enjoyed babysitting our grandchildren together—we were a good team. Tyson stayed connected to us. He felt like family, and I couldn't imagine losing another family member. We talked on the phone, sometimes meeting for dinner or visiting him at his apartment by UCLA. He kept us updated on life and told us when he felt he was ready to date. We were honored. When we chatted and asked him for details about his dates, he said they were ok, but that was all. He never told us any names.

In the ensuing months, we still got calls, and during one, Tyson talked on and on about a date he had with a girl he met at church. Before long, he called again with new energy in his voice.

"I'd really like you to meet Laura," he said.

Diana

Michael Daniel Spencer. Sometimes just saying his name brings tears. He came 5 1/2 years after Gabriel was born. He was very tender-hearted from the start—loving, kind—and as he got older, developed an incredible sense of humor.

At 14, a friend introduced him to pot. He loved it from the get-go. Michael later told his dad and me that smoking pot made him feel like his real self. He said it made him fit in like he was an equal. He began drinking as well. We knew something was off when Mike began to be gone more. He seemed more aloof, which was not typical. This was not his real self.

More and more, we saw signs that he wasn't just experimenting or using it occasionally. And, more and more, I felt the shock that Michael had no desire to quit drinking and quit smoking pot. It seemed so obvious to me that the reason for such discord, anger, and unhappiness—in himself and us—was his using.

I got stuck for a while in my line of thinking—How could this happen in our family? What did we do wrong? I thought we were a close-knit family, and now I felt like we failed as parents. I thought we'd been doing it right. We were involved in church and Bible studies; both sons were a part of the church youth group. I prayed.... a lot. I'd been part of a "Moms in Touch" group and was a volunteer pastor for high school students. You see, I had this false idea about God, that he rewards those who do it 'right'. Right, according to me, of course.

By the end of 10th grade, we decided to move Michael to a Christian high school. It seemed like his mood improved, his desire to be around us improved, and his grades improved. I definitely thought he'd stopped using. But this was not the case. He had simply learned how to hide his use better. Mike wanted to return to the public high school for his senior year because he and most of his friends had gone to the same school since grade school. His friends were really great kids...just like Michael. Things seemed okay at first, but I started to notice some strange habits. He would stay up very late, 3 or 4 in the morning. I tried to give Mike "helpful" advice on the need for sleep. One night, I saw the light in his bathroom and debated opening the door. With no noise or movement inside, I cracked the door only to see him splayed out cold on the floor. On the vanity counter were all sorts of hard liquor bottles. And, oh boy, I knew we were in trouble.

The friend who introduced Michael to pot had gone to rehab the year before. Honestly, we didn't know whether that was right for Mike or what we should do. We felt a desperation to get him help, in any case. Fear and sadness weighed very heavily on me. We hired a professional interventionist. Mike had turned eighteen a few months prior to this. If he did not want to go to rehab, we could not force him. But he said yes. Michael went to rehab in Utah for five weeks. It was a wilderness retreat in Utah. I drove him to the airport, along with the interventionist who would accompany him to the facility. I hugged Mike for so long and so hard. I was emotionally and totally distraught. I felt like I was not up to this 'sending Mike away' situation!! I actually felt like I didn't want to live anymore. During those weeks, while he was gone, I remember feeling obsessed and consumed with thoughts of Michael. Will this rehab 'fix him'? Is he okay? Is he warm? Is he angry with us?

When we went to retrieve him as a family, he looked great. He seemed like the Michael we knew to be Michael. It was at that time that Mike told us he was an alcoholic. The therapists advised us not to bring him back to our home because he was new in his recovery. We were told it was not good to put him in an old environment where we were still the same. I had a lot of anger toward that whole ideal. Mike made it clear he wanted to come home, and I wanted him home. Again, I felt the crushing weight of sadness. And I feared for Mike's feelings—his desire to come home and us saying no! It was dreadful!

Michael moved into a sober living facility not that far from us. He was clean and sober and worked a 12-step program for ten months. I had a hard time visiting the home he stayed in. It seemed so harsh, so many people, so many beds close together. I never drove back home without at least once pulling over to the side of the road, crying so hard I couldn't see through my overflowing sorrow. I so desperately wanted this to be over. I wanted Mike home, I wanted my family whole and healthy, and I wanted us back together.

But he seemed to be doing well, and soon, he moved into an apartment with two of the guys from the sober living home. I thought this was great—he was making progress growing up. But by age 21, we knew he was definitely back to drinking and smoking. He lost his license to drive at one point, but we never found out the reason. He began using public transportation. For the next ten years of his life, he would take the bus everywhere he needed to go.

Michael was a food server and a very good one, much loved by customers. But his unreliability would eventually get him fired, and he'd have to go to another restaurant. It would be an argument with a cook or a bad attitude, but he was always changing jobs. At one point, he got arrested. He was very drunk on his way home from the bus stop when he went into the back door of Mimi's restaurant. The front door was closed, but their kitchen door wasn't locked, so he decided to go in and make himself a sandwich. The police came and arrested him.

During the time Michael was 21-30 years, we seemed to hear about new incidents and new paradigms to wrap our minds around.

My husband and I had been encouraged to try Al-Anon when Mike went to the first rehab. We did try, and we stayed. It changed my life profoundly. Here was a group of people that understood. They had people they loved in their lives, and they couldn't fix them. This is where I learned to pray the serenity prayer: "God, grant me the serenity to accept the things I cannot change (people), the courage to change the things I can (me!), and the wisdom to know the difference." Living one day at a time. Enjoying one moment at a time. Accepting hardship as the pathway to peace. Taking, as Jesus did, this sinful world not as I would have it, trusting that He will make all things right if I surrender to His will, that I may be reasonably happy in this life and supremely happy with Him forever in the next. Amen."

The kingdom of God was displayed in such a tangible way there, boots on the ground/rubber meet the road kind of ways. It was life-changing, the unconditional love and compassion that was displayed. But more than that, I was discovering solutions for myself. When I first walked into an Al-Anon meeting, I was in despair. I could not see how I could be happy and believed serenity was a pipe dream!

I was raised by Christian parents, and somewhere along the way, I'd picked up the idea that 'things will go well with you if you do everything right.' A holy tit for tat, I guess. So, with that mentality, I presumed that my husband and I had caused Michael's disease, adding disappointment and shame to an already heavy burden. What had I done wrong to end up here? It did not occur to me that our son, like me, has the freedom before God to make his own choices and walk his own way. Christian families are not immune to the world's suffering.

There was a side of me that slowly woke up. Al-Anon helped me put words to my feelings. When I heard other parents share their hearts, I would say, I'm feeling that too. But I hadn't found the right words to verbalize till then. Now, I saw others who had experienced or were experiencing pain and loss and yet found a way to be happy, hopeful and encouraged. So, I learned to let go of my expectations, anger, and disappointment.

We went to a parent focus Al-Anon meeting for 14 years. During this time, I heard the stories of at least five moms or dads whose sons or daughters had died from the disease. It was always shocking to hear these stories. I simply could not imagine, and I never did imagine that would EVER happen to Michael.

I also learned I had to focus on my own thoughts and actions. I quickly realized that I had been obsessing about what others should be doing, especially those closest to me! Christ became so much bigger to me. Day by day, I made the decision to turn my will over to God. I turned my will—that Michael finds recovery—over to God. Michael was also given the gift of a will too. I was not in charge of Mike's will! It was *his* to manage. I had to let Mike be who he was and love him for just that. He was a grown man, and whether I thought what he was doing was unhealthy or unhelpful, it was not my right to control his environment. My love had been conditional, and that had to change. I had to find a new way to respect and honor the dignity of Michael. God was with Mike, as well as me.

But we had to have boundaries in our life, too. If he was visiting, he had to remain sober. One day, I came home when Michael was visiting for a couple days, and I saw him outside hiding in the bushes. Not a sight you want to see with your grown son. He saw me and went into the garage. I met him in the garage. I knew he was drunk. I told him I loved him, I believed in him, and I trusted him to make the best choices for himself. But I also told him he couldn't stay here using substances. These moments were very, very hard for me. I offered to drive him where he needed to go. He kindly declined my offer. He got his backpack and walked off, probably to the bus stop. Although these times felt awful, they gave me the opportunity to express my love and confidence in him and that he would make the best choice for himself.

Psalm 16 was helpful during these days, especially in the nighttime when I wondered if Michael was on the streets. "I have set the Lord always before me; because he is at my right hand, I shall not be shaken." The 23rd Psalm was always a comfort. I had memorized Psalm 145, "The Lord upholds all who are falling and raises all who are bowed down." So comforting and hopeful. The Serenity Prayer was crucial for me. The hardest

line for me was, "Accepting hardship as a pathway to peace."
And yet that line was the most life changing.

During one visit with Mike in our home, he told his dad that he
believed he was constitutionally incapable of being honest with
himself. That was a sad moment for me, for us. We knew he was
quoting from a reading from Alcoholics Anonymous, which is
read in many AA meetings - "Rarely have we seen a person fail
who has thoroughly followed our path. Those who do not
recover are people who cannot or will not completely give
themselves to this simple program—usually men and women
who are constitutionally incapable of being honest with
themselves. There are such unfortunates. They are not at fault;
they seem to have been born that way. They are naturally
incapable of grasping and developing a manner of living that
demands rigorous honesty. Their chances are less than
average." These are the addicts who have the most difficulty
achieving successful sobriety. I asked my husband if he told
Michael he was wrong about himself, that he *could* be honest
with himself. My husband said he just listened. I was so angry! I
felt my husband had missed the perfect opportunity to set
Mike's thinking straight. And there I was: trying to control
things, not accepting the will of my son. Or my husband. Trying
to fix this.

I had to become comfortable with 'the news, weather, and
sports'. Michael wanted to connect with us, and we wanted to
connect with him! When he was sober and in recovery, we had
great conversations about recovery, about family, about 'life'.
But when he was drinking or using, it was not possible to have a
conversation that was, for lack of a better phrase, meaningful.
We choose to be comfortable and okay with the superficial. I'd
go to open AA meetings. I pictured Mike's face in the different
young people sharing. I heard from them what a challenge it
was to stay sober. I also heard the miracles in recovery. I knew
that these were the people that could help my son. It released
any illusion that the help would come from me. I never heard in
an AA meeting testimony, "My mom got me sober."

But Mike was getting sicker. He'd been in jail three times and rehab three times. I always thought he was going to make it. Always! After every rehab, the counselors felt Michael would make it.

It was 6:30 AM on a Friday morning, and I was talking to my twin sister on the phone when I heard my husband answer his phone and begin to wail like I'd never heard before. I broke off my call because I'd thought my husband's mom had died. But no….

Michael was dead. His roommate had called and told us that Mike had hung himself. I found myself screaming in indescribable agony. I just couldn't accept this. Just seven days before, we had had such a great time together with his nephew. Mike told us he was finally getting his license back. He had just told of his hope that his life was coming together.

We drove to the house where he was renting a room. The authorities were already there. There were two grief counselors. We had no idea how they knew or who told them to be there. They were there just to hold us and console us. They were wonderful and gentle. We called Gabriel and our families. Gabe came over and told us that there was no way that Michael had hung himself intentionally. They had just been playing a game over the phone at 4 AM that morning, and Mike was coming over to his house later that day. It wasn't suicide. He had not hung himself. It was an asphyxiation rush that had gone too far. Just another popular way of getting high these days, we learned. His roommate, who found Michael, did not want to tell us how he died for fear we would somehow think it was worse. Mike had been drinking incredible amounts of alcohol that night. They found his bathrobe tie laying over his shoulder, and police assumed he'd used it to temporarily strangle himself for the 'high' it provides, but his extreme alcohol impairment let it go too far.

A friend of a friend from Saddleback Church was at our house when we drove back. She was amazing. She had been a help to others who had experienced such profound loss. We did not know we were in shock. She did. We did not know we were the ones to call whoever took Michael's body so we could get his body released to the mortuary. She did. She made the arrangements to get Michael released to the mortuary that very day. At 6 pm, we drove to the mortuary, and I could not stop shaking. When I saw him at the mortuary, he looked beautiful. Peaceful. But he was cold. I wailed and wailed and wailed.

I begged him to come back to us. I had this unreasonable sense that he could come back. I had no problem falling to the ground in travail. I did that a lot. The grief felt unbearable.

I was so blessed that I had people I could call at 4 AM to talk and cry to. Death just seemed so unnatural to me. I knew Michael was in a much better place, and of course, I knew I would see him again. But Mike not being here – no, no, no, no, no!!!!! I was virulently angry with God for months. I couldn't pray or study. We didn't go to church. I reverted to, "Look at all the changes I've made, God. Look at all the work I've been doing. WHY???"

I lost interest in food. Nothing tasted good. I remember having to go to the store and being shocked, almost paralyzed, that people seemed to be going on as if nothing had happened. But for me, everything was different. How did they all not know that something cataclysmic had happened? I had no idea what to tell people. A few days after Mike died, a couple showed up at our door who had lost their son two years prior came. They told us that this time had to be all about us. This was our time to grieve, and we couldn't be responsible for other people's feelings. It was such a release and freedom because I truly didn't have the energy and capacity to help anyone else.

I had decided to go through and clean some of Mike's things out. But it was too soon. As I pulled out an old backpack, I found a bus pass. It hit me like a tidal wave. My chest hurt so bad, and I sobbed—a heart fracturing, head hurting, soul aching flood. I called a friend who had been in AA for years. I don't totally understand why I called him. I think I needed to hear from another alcoholic that the disease of alcoholism is brutal. The pain, guilt, and grief came pouring out of me. He understood. He was so kind. He suggested I stop trying to 'clean' this cupboard for now and put the stuff away. Maybe wait a little while. I realized then that I had to face this grief head-on. I couldn't clean it all away. But with the kindness and help of these friends, this grief wouldn't consume me. So, I started reading. And writing.

My relationship with God began to grow again as I came across some classical works of art, especially religious art. I focused on the detail and emotion the artist found in Christ on earth and in Mary, his mother. It brought me closer to understanding Christ's love and sacrifice and the human pain his mother, Mary, must have endured. The disciples in the boat where Christ slept as the storm raged gave me much to ponder. In a journal, I wrote…

> "One man appears to be leaning over the rail…Despairing? Heaving? His hands on his head, 'This is too much to take in?' He's in darkness, waiting it out, enduring. But Jesus is enduring the storm, too. He stays in the boat throughout the tempest. Please, Jesus, stop the storm! It's too much. Jesus the one who is God. God with us. Not a distant God ruling the universe from out there. He's here in my midst, in the middle of the storm." —Diana

Michael's death transformed us. We are better people for having known and loved Mike and better people for having walked this road of suffering. We have a greater capacity for empathy and can ask people honestly, "How are you doing *today*?" And every time we see Bus #89 roll by our house, we pray for the riders and the driver that God would be present in their lives and that they will make the best choices for themselves.

A family member said to me that it was God's will, that God had planned to take Mike early. But I reject that. I don't think it was God's will at all. I don't think God planned for Michael to die at 30. I think God knew and knew all the possible choices Mike could make. And I believe that God had already made plans and provisions for every scenario that could have happened. I think

He is the absolute smartest, most creative being in the universe. For Him to see all the possibilities of what Mike could do is nothing to him. It is not hard for him. I found great comfort in the fact that God loved Michael and was right there with Michael as life left him. I also believe God profoundly grieved with us.

As I watched Mike slowly kill himself, I learned much more about what was going on inside of me and gained a willingness to be transparent to safe people; to share my fears and brokenness with others. I do not doubt that Mike is now happy, productive, and free, doing what God intended into the fullness that is Michael.

From my journal …

"There is a sense that God is hiding, and yet I have peeked glory in what we are given. I've seen it on your faces and felt it in the long, lingering hugs. I've watched how duties and responsibilities have been dropped to carry our family as we try so hard to make it one hour at a time, as we say to each other, 'We made it one more day without Michael'. *Thank you* seems completely inadequate for what we are given. What we are given is truly life support." — Diana

Leigh Ann

Elizabeth was our first and only child—not trying, little miracle. It was a normal pregnancy. But on one of the exams, the doctor said, "This is going to be one big baby!" No one was concerned as my husband, Roger, is a very large man in height and breadth. But right at term, they did an ultrasound and discovered Elizabeth's head was extremely large and then discovered she was hydrocephalic (water on the brain). They said the chances of her surviving the birth were slim. I called Roger, and by the time he walked into the doctor's office, I was already hysterical.

They scheduled a C-section. The staff told us we would need Medi-Cal coverage if she did survive. Roger and I talked about it, and they scheduled counseling. I was so traumatized and felt no amount of talking would help. I could still feel my baby moving and just wanted to give birth regardless of the outcome. C-section day came, and when they pulled her out, she began to cry. It was such a huge rollercoaster—preparing for loss, then preparing for…???

Neither of us could hold her because of the size and precarious nature of her head. But her daddy's first comment— "Oh, she is sooo beautiful!" And you knew he meant it with every measure of his soul. She was already daddy's girl. Roger's mom whispered, "He doesn't see it, the size of her head." My mom replied," No, he doesn't. That's his child, and he loves her."

Elizabeth was then put in an incubator and sent to the University of California Irvine Medical Center. The following day, a shunt was put in to drain the spinal fluid from her brain. The experts were always skeptical and gave us little hope of Elizabeth surviving. She wasn't supposed to survive birth; she wasn't supposed to survive for the entire two weeks. But she continued to mock them by simply living and improving.

I was stuck at the hospital recovering and didn't get to see her for a week. But daddy went with her and reported to me, taking Polaroids daily. As the fluid lessened down to 2 lbs., Elizabeth's skull plates came down and somewhat overlapped, giving her a ridge. They had grown large to compensate for the fluid. But she began to progress. Everything seemed to be going well, and we brought her home.

We lived with my parents at the time—a mutual survival situation—but it was a blessing. If the baby cried in the middle of the night, my dad and mom were there before we even got to her. My dad truly cherished her. Before Elizabeth came into our world, Dad had lost hope in life due to crushing losses: the sudden end of a major government career and the sudden death of his only son, my brother. Dad was barely breathing, hardly surviving. Elizabeth gave him purpose again. His love and commitment to her were instant and profound.

At three months, Elizabeth was doing well, healing and progressing. She was only slightly behind in development. But our optimism was short-lived. Multiple shunt failures prevented spinal fluid from draining, clogging flow from her brain, sending us to the hospital every weekend. The shunt required manual pumping, done by a horde of different resident MDs. We were sent home on Mondays— doctors giving the 'all clear, everything's fine'—only to have to race back by Friday. The shunt failures manifested into meningitis and peritonitis. Elizabeth was very sick, and the doctors didn't think she would survive. Again. But by

God's merciful grace, she lived on, tackling many new complications. Seizures, for one. There were lots of pediatricians who didn't know what to do with her, and many panicked. What was I supposed to do if they didn't know, me a lowly first-time mom?

There were a few other parents with hydrocephalic children of differing severity that we'd met, but each case was so different, ranging in manifestations. We still created great bonds with these families. We could understand them, and they could understand our trauma. In some ways, we were all a training ground for these doctors. One doctor asked me if I had taken her temperature orally. I think my head spun completely around. With her seizures and unpredictable movements, I quipped, "Why yes, doctor, I feed my child mercury every day." Snort. You are not touching my child, I mused. I really had to learn how to advocate for Elizabeth; I think we all found our voices through her. She brought our family so close, and she brought the neighborhood around us together. Everyone was there for love and support. We all came to realize how precious and tenuous life is.

After the infection subsided, Elizabeth was still having seizures, but she was home and finally able to go to an early development program. She got help with fine motor skills, occupational therapy, and socialization. But the infections and the seizures profoundly altered the developmental trajectory she had been on before meningitis and peritonitis. We put her on that little yellow bus for many years, several times a week. She learned to say "Hi" to everyone, and she would sing the "Jeopardy" theme song. (I think Grandma's viewing habits had something to do with that.) She developed a small vocabulary, probably 30 words maximum. At ten, the child that shouldn't have survived birth was given a communication device on the computer, and she got very good at it. We found a deep sense of humor within her through this device. She was able to ask her cousin, "What size bowl did you use for that haircut?" And she kept hitting the repeat button throughout his visit.

I had to be the mommy— "Don't do this. Don't do that. Don't think you can get away with this because you're special. Yes, you're special, but you still can't do that." Those kinds of things were my world with Elizabeth. I took her to therapy and doctor appointments. This allowed Roger to be the daddy he was designed to be, ever-loving and forgiving. He catered to and nurtured; loved to take her shopping. The "Limited 2" was a favorite destination; he would always engage the girls working the floor to find Elizabeth the cute, stylish clothes. Roger read the book *Plan B: What Do You Do When God Doesn't Show Up the Way You Thought He Would* by *Pete Wilson*. He really took it to heart and made every second with Elizabeth count.

Other than parents in the hospital and therapy, I found that attending support groups was not helpful. I couldn't dwell on what might happen or how bad things could get. I needed to stay hopeful and positive, and it worked for me. I don't discount the groups for others. Everyone must find what works for them. We did find a Hydrocephalic group out of the hospital that was piloted by our neurosurgeon's assistant. It was great while it lasted, but when the leader moved, the group just disbanded.

Through Miller's Children's Hospital, we finally found a competent pediatrician, neurologist, and neurosurgeon— all the things Elizabeth needed. They did so many tests and scans to see if they could curb her seizures which all stemmed from meningitis. They did surgery to separate the two hemispheres in her brain to mitigate the seizures.

She was a little 'zipperhead,' and it worked incredibly well for six weeks. She was walking and moving much better, but after six weeks, the brain learned how to overcome the surgery, and the seizures returned.

All the seizures weakened her left side, and so scoliosis began leaning her to the left. It became so bad that she only had 30% lung capacity in her left lung. Her rib cage was basically hitting her left hip bone, and the only specialties Miller's didn't have were good orthopedists. Elizabeth needed back surgery to straighten her spine and relieve the strain on her left side. This led us to a 'lovely' doctor at another facility. After just a few minutes, this condescending surgeon blurted, "Well, how is back surgery going to make her a more contributing member of society?!" I thought my husband was going to beat the record in the long jump, leaping over the desk to strangle him. Imagine a 6'4', 290lb. angry dad who adores his daughter, hurtling over your fancy, minimalist, shiny glass desk with Thor hands reaching for your throat. I think Dr. Quack got the image, too.

As I calmed Roger down, I began my own offense on the 'good' doctor for that comment. I thought of every stupid question I could ask and wasted over an hour of his self-important time. Jackhole. Needless-to-say, he was not touching my child. We found a great orthopedic spine surgeon in downtown LA.

However, during the very delicate surgery, when the doctor put the rods in Elizabeth's back, the sensors on her spine went flat, and he was afraid he'd paralyzed her. We knew how risky the surgery was, but on seeing the surgeon's face when he came to share the results, we prepared for the worst. The doctor himself was so bereft and remorseful as he took us to recovery to see our girl.

But once again, the girl who wouldn't survive surprised us all by moving her foot. The relief on the doctor's face was even brighter than ours.

The surgery improved Elizabeth's breathing but impeded her movement as she had stiff rods in her back, so she had another learning curve to hurdle. At home, she was pretty much bound to her fancy stroller with head supports. At school, they had systems to get them up and out of their chairs, holding them vertically and getting some much-needed weight-bearing exercise. As well as means to shower and use the restroom.

Elizabeth had such a will to survive, but she was stubborn too. She only wanted to do what she wanted to do. Fortunately, I was more stubborn. I saw the pitfalls for some parents with special needs, the choice to not expect much from their child and let them be couch potatoes. Once they realized their child would not be collegiate or an athlete, many gave up and coddled too much. I found that special needs kids have a purpose. They change hearts and minds around them, bringing the best out of family, friends, and neighbors to make the world a better place. I wanted to make sure Elizabeth could fulfill the time-honored cliché—be the best she could be.

Elizabeth was now a teenager and in a high school program. We had moved to La Habra, CA, and put her in a program in Brea. Her seizures were less severe and more controlled, so her communication and socialization improved. The high school kids and college kids from Cal State Fullerton would come into the classrooms to help, and CSF hosted the Special Olympics, which they all got to participate in. There was so much activity and stimulation that Elizabeth's communication and alertness improved.

She loved hanging out with kids outside of her normal classmates.

Elizabeth also had a nurse who was raising her own granddaughter, and she would keep her for some weekends so that Roger and I got much-needed time as a couple. It's hard to unwind yourself from the 24/7 needs of a child like Elizabeth because neither of us wanted to detach from her. But we realized it was important to be a couple, to be an us, and in the end, it's probably what saved us.

Now being in a neighborhood, Elizabeth gained a friend, Samantha, who then brought her gal pals too. Soon, our house was full of giggling girls who talked and whirled around our daughter. She felt like the queen and loved every minute.

By Elizabeth's 17th year, we were still managing her seizures, but she was doing well medically. Roger wanted to apply to the Make-A-Wish Foundation before her 18th birthday. When she was small, Elizabeth loved the tropical climate when we took her to Hawaii, so her dad thought she would love swimming with the dolphins. The foundation found a program in Key Largo, FL, with a weeklong program, and they made it happen. Elizabeth had a ball. She even ended up with a crush on her therapist. He was very sensitive and sweet but had to let her down, informing her that he couldn't have relationships with clients. We ended up taking her every year for seven years. The girl who wouldn't survive had girlfriends had a crush and swam with dolphins.

The program became a great motivational tool for me, too. When she was stubborn or lethargic, I could just say, "How are you going to hold on to Squirt's dorsal fin if you can't even hold onto this fork/baton/paintbrush/fill in the blank? It was really great for me—a determined mom—to have such a strong motivational tool. Call me wicked, but Elizabeth really progressed.

We also found a new neurologist who could find the right cocktail to reduce her seizures from several a day to once a month. But her inability to move with the rods in her back left her more vulnerable to things like pneumonia after colds—another battleground for me. But we found sunshine days within it. Elizabeth would have to wear a compression vest and be hooked to a nebulizer. She looked like a space animal, and I would get the giggles. "Look at your schnout there, Elizabeth! Hahahaha." Boy, the look I got was a typical mother-daughter moment. Mooother!!

Elizabeth graduated from her high school program at 21, and we celebrated at a bowling alley—her choice. We all had so much fun. Now she was off to another program only 8 miles from our house. But she kept getting pneumonia, needing breathing treatments, making her attendance sketchy.

My dad passed away when Elizabeth was 24. That was a rough passage. And yet it was beautiful. All those friends, neighbors, and acquaintances at the service watched this severely disabled young woman hang her head over the casket, so close to her grandfather, and tenderly stroke his face. She knew who he was, she knew what he meant to her, and she knew his life had filled her with unconditional love. All lives do matter. This loss was hard for me, too. My relationship with my dad and Elizabeth's relationship with her grandpa was just so special. As I watched her mourn, my own cheeks were wet with memories of late nights hanging over Elizabeth's crib, my dad calming her back to sleep after seizures or a rough night. This was a hard goodbye. But looking back, my dad would not have survived what was to come two years later.

Elizabeth began dealing with breathing issues and pneumonia on a regular basis. I guess if I'd thought hard enough about it, I'd have realized how much pain they caused her. But I was too focused, frantically helping get her lungs clear so she could breathe.

One Sunday morning, I bounced out of bed at 6 am. On weekend mornings, I don't bounce. But for some reason, this morning, I did. I went into Elizabeth, now 26, to get her up and dressed and give her a breathing treatment. She had just had a checkup from her pulmonary specialist, and everything seemed to be good. Looking back, the doc and I think Elizabeth manipulated her test. It's possible to get a false reading if you know when to breathe and when to hold your breath, which spoke volumes of Elizabeth's intelligence. I checked her oxygen saturation rate and blanched. It was bad and going down.

I tested it again and yelled for Roger to call the paramedics. The dog was racing around frantic, I was trying to do a breathing treatment, and Roger went out to wait for the paramedics. I felt so alone in the middle of so much chaos. But I needed to keep focused on the task at hand. When I looked down at Elizabeth, a single tear was running down her cheek. And then she lost consciousness. I started doing CPR immediately as the police arrived but still no paramedics. In actuality, it didn't take them long, but when seconds matter, it felt like forever before they arrived.

Elizabeth usually liked the attention when the paramedics were called. All those cute men hovering around her giving her attention and the life-giving aid she needed. But not today. Today was different.

The police asked if Elizabeth was in Hospice, and I rudely blurted, "No!!" So, they took over doing CPR. So many questions were being thrown at me, and all I could think about was saving my child's life. When the paramedics arrived and handled the equipment, I instantly assessed everything I was doing wrong and started the personal blame game. I was mad at the police, frustrated with Roger—where was he? Finally, it got sorted out, and Roger rode with the paramedics to the hospital while I followed in the car. I was driving hysterically, and luckily, I didn't get pulled over. But I was in no rush to get to the hospital. Somewhere deep inside, I knew what awaited me.

I fought with the reception to get back to the emergency, and I wasn't taking any attitude. When I did get back, they were still working on my girl. Elizabeth had not regained consciousness, and the doctor asked us what we wanted to do. I kept thinking of Elizabeth's last expression and the pain-filled tear, and I knew. Roger and I were just very quiet. Eventually, her death was called, and they gave us time to be with her. I focused on her eyes and her skin, just touching her. I wanted to hold her and take it all in for the last time. There's a connectedness special needs parents have with their children that others do not. I mean, who gets to spend every day with their teenager, so closely bonded? They are so dependent that the kinship is stronger every day of their life. Letting go is so much harder.

At the service, one of the eulogists shared about 'dying grace'. Elizabeth had been given her 'dying grace' ticket and passed peacefully into eternity. When we watch others suffer such great loss, we think we couldn't possibly go through what they are experiencing. What they don't realize is that they haven't been given a 'suffering grace' ticket. It's like a ticket to go on a trip. You don't get it till you need it. God gives you 'suffering grace' when tragedy befalls you. That's what we had, and that's how we muddled through.

The service wasn't hard to arrange; we used the same folks that had done my dad two years prior. We wore bright colors because that's what Elizabeth liked. It was a light-hearted couple of days with good friends circling around. But there were times I would head to the garage by myself and just wail.

After the ceremonies, the first thing I did was purge the house of all things medical because that wasn't who Elizabeth was. Her nurse was very upset with Elizabeth's passing and came over to help us, just doing physical things. I wanted to get rid of the hard parts and remember the good parts. We donated her health supplies and even found a home for her wheelchair that could be attached to a surfboard.

There was a grief counseling group through the mortuary. Roger and I were placed in different groups so we could be brutally honest without worrying about the feelings of the person we faced every day. They gave us books to read. Roger really loved *Good Grief* by *Granger E. Westberg*. *The Grief Recovery Handbook by John W. James and Russel Friedman* was helpful, too. The group prepared us for constructive conversations with each other.

For a while, I struggled to find purpose. Elizabeth had been my sole direction and effort. Everything seemed so trivial compared to life with my daughter. She was a miracle, a gift from God, and I spent so much time in gratitude for every minute we had with her. Her nurse, Kathie, is still a dear friend, more like a big sister to me. And our friends have been patient and welcoming of conversation about our sweet girl. It's taken me many years to find my childless way and what God had planned for me after Elizabeth. But he had not punched my ticket, so I had to move forward. I found the first step—getting my graduate degree.

I had a recent dream of Elizabeth. She was giving me a tour of where she was living now. It was heaven, and she was so joyful, so whole.

The girl who wouldn't survive lived a happy, loving 26 years on this earth. A life well-lived, well-loved who left everyone she met, changed for the better. Now she lives for eternity, swimming in unimaginable beauty.

And when my 'dying ticket' comes, I will dive in and float alongside her.

Jami

I was a teen mom, and my little girl was Vada. She was my little baby doll. But I was still a kid in my mind, not having experienced the things I'd wanted to experience. Vada's father was my high school boyfriend, but he was a hippie and a loadie. At first, he tried to be involved a little, occasionally sending Vada dresses on birthdays and Christmas. But he drifted away, which was fine with me. I had a hard time sharing her.

We lived with my parents, and she became the family baby; my mom taught me everything. It was beautiful and challenging, yet heartbreaking at times. I had other plans, but God made me a mom. My life revolved around Vada, and she was my little best friend. But we were both kind of lost. I was lucky to know God and got us to church, but there was still a pull on me to do the things my friends were doing. So, on weekends, my parents took over so I could. I fell into a dark place, trying to live in two different worlds. It couldn't go on, so I recommitted to a Christian lifestyle. If I was going to find a proper family life and dad for Vada, I had to get myself right with the Lord.

I was working as a bartender at the time, and after work, I stopped at another hangout. This guy John was there hanging out with friends. We got to talking and found so many things in common, especially a life centered on God, and we attended similar-style churches. But he said he was on probation, and I was hesitant—not sure what that meant. I told my mom I had met this perfect guy, but he was on probation. John called soon after to ask me on a date, and in the conversation, I learned his probation period was part of his training to be a fireman.

He was perfect, after all! And he wasn't intimidated in the least that I had a child. After that date, we spent every single day together. And we did it right; we didn't sleep together or live together. When he met my little 2-year-old girl, he became her dad. They bonded so quickly, and he's the only dad she knows. He was very, very good to her. Being a dad came naturally to him. When he proposed to me, he proposed to Vada, and we got married a month later—three years after we met. We had a Christian ceremony at the beach, and we started our life devoted to God and each other and the church community.

Shortly after we were married, we were pregnant. Other than some morning sickness, which I had with Vada, it was a perfect pregnancy. We brought blue balloons to our parents to announce we were having a boy. They were excited, and we were excited—it was such a joyous time for this close-knit Italian family. Our boy was to have the Sicilian name Gaetano. This was John's dad's name, and he was jubilant; he acted like he'd won the lottery.

 My John was so excited to have a boy, but I was scared because all I knew were girls: mom, sisters, and my little Vada. The morning sickness was a stressor, but it eased up after about five months. We lived near the beach, so we made Gaetano's nursery a beach theme, but there was also a fire truck and soccer ball thrown in for flavor. We found this quote online, "If you want to know how much I love you, just count the waves in the sea." I loved it and had it blown up and framed to hang over Gaetano's crib. I loved secondhand stores, so I shopped to distract myself from the morning sickness. This baby had a closet full of clothes and 20 pairs of shoes before there was even a baby shower. It was such a happy time. Vada loved the nursery and would play with her dolls and rock them in the nursery rocking chair. My baby girl was a natural nurturer.

All our doctor appointments were awesome. Every ultrasound showed a big, strong, thriving, healthy baby—thick arms and legs and full lips. He loved music and would always move to the radio or worship songs at church.

We were a couple days from his due date when I became particularly nauseous and sensed decreased movement with Gaetano. I had the sitter watch Vada so I could get to a doctor. I went straight to the hospital, where they did an ultrasound and ran a stress test. We listened to the heartbeat, and the technician said all was well. They wanted me to sign the yellow paper that stated that I was confident to leave the hospital, but I just couldn't. My instinct told me that 'all was not well.' They kept pushing me to sign this, to release me, but I was still hesitant. I was still young and insecure, but they assured me, so I went home to be with my family.

We were celebrating our year anniversary with everyone: cutting up the wedding cake, watching the wedding video, and toasting a wondrous first year. Gaetano must have been celebrating, too, because he was dancing on my insides like mad. It was such a happy night.

John's sister made us a Pizookie—a hot chocolate chip cookie topped with ice cream. She tended to undercook things, so I teased her, saying that if that thing was not cooked thoroughly and I got sick, and something happened to the baby, I'd be coming after her. We all laughed. I didn't mean anything by it, but I was pretty restless that night, and Gaetano was bouncing around inside me. I was nauseous and had acid reflux, and I was extremely uncomfortable with this full-sized big boy pummeling my uterine walls. I sat in the rocking chair of the nursery and felt a sharp twinge. But it passed, and the baby was still moving as I fell asleep in the chair.

We got up the next morning and went to church. During the worship songs, Gaetano wasn't moving. That was unusual. At first, I thought it was our late night with all the food and activity, and he was finally sleeping. John thought the same, so we went to have some Mexican food. Still no movement. I called the nurse, and she said to have a Slurpee. Weird, but we went to 7/11, got Slurpees, and went home for a nap. After lying down for a while, I grabbed John's hand and had him feel my belly.

"The baby is not moving."

So, John took us to the hospital. It was Gaetano's due date, and we assumed it was just time for him to come out. It took us a while to get in, but we were finally escorted into the room for ultrasounds. The nurse prepped me and started watching the monitor. She was very quiet, and the room was so quiet as she scanned the monitor, eyes squinting.

We start to ask questions: 'What's going on?' 'How's he doing?'

She turned to us and said, "I think we need to move. This machine's broken."

So, she rolls up another machine and starts the test again. After a few minutes, she said she wanted to call the doctor because she didn't think this machine was working either. (We learned later that they do this broken ultrasound shuffle with everyone in our situation because the technician is not allowed to tell you anything.) But the doctor took forever, so we started pelting the tech with questions.

"You look really worried. Is there a heartbeat? What's going on?"

She finally admitted that she was not allowed to tell us any details of our condition. But the doctor was taking forever to get there, so she told us that she was allowed to put down the wand if there was no heartbeat. She checked my abdomen one more time, set down the wand, and walked out of the room.

I remember going into complete shock. John was so distraught that he melted, then struck out and punched a hole in the wall. He marched out to the waiting room, yelling at everyone for making us wait so long—they were at fault. I was still in shock but realized I had to be the strong one right now because John had completely lost it. I went out, got him to stop, and pulled him back to the room, blocking the door.

 So, John called his dad, who was heading into the Grammy Awards with a friend of his. He was so pumped and excited to step into the venue. When John didn't respond to his dad's excitement, he started questioning and inquiring.

"It's not good, not good, Dad. It's not good at all."

John told him the news, and his dad started screaming and screaming right there on the red carpet. He left, never making it into the awards ceremony. The family was more important.

We held onto each other in that room and just called family. We needed them; we needed people. Hardly anyone was available, but I finally found my sister-in-law. And she was a saint, our eclectic tattoo-covered angel. She said she'd get a hold of everyone and would be at the hospital soon.

Still no doctor. I think they were giving us time to process, but we're still of a mindset that something could be done.

Nurses would briefly check-in, but many were hesitant from John's outburst. Finally, a doctor came, not our doctor but a doctor. He gave his condolences and offered us two choices. You can deliver the baby or have a c-section. My immediate thought was c-section. I was angry at the thought of delivering a dead baby. But a couple of nurses trained for this purpose explained that delivering the baby helps you get through the grieving process. The labor, delivery, and holding of the baby help move you to finality with your child. In their experience, they'd witnessed the full delivery process as the best way. And the sooner, the better, as the baby would still look angelic and lifelike.

And so, we did. They induced me and put me in a different room, but it was a sad little room designed for this purpose. We were still on the delivery floor, so we could hear other babies crying and families cheering as babies were born. Our room had a leaf on the wall with a tear dropping down. This notified delivery nurses that this was a special mom and a special delivery. Nurses came in and out, John came in and out, but they put our families in a room next door. Our friends came, and half of the fire department came and parked a fire truck near the room. Folks would occasionally come in our room, not say much, give a kiss on the head, touch my belly, and leave. I was alone a lot in that room. Visitors seemed to treat me like I was dying too. And maybe I was, the emotional part of me.

John was in the other room most of the time, processing. He's a people person who needed them to process his grieving. This was devastating for him. And my room was just an empty, dismal room. The nurses were great, and at one point, they had two ladies come to visit. They were photographers and asked if we would like photos when the baby came. My first thought was, 'No. That's so morbid.

How could you take pictures of a dead baby?' They were kind and considerate, leaving me to myself. Soon, one of the grief nurses who had advised me to deliver the baby came in and advised me to have the pictures taken.

"They're beautiful and very tastefully done, and you're going to want to have them to commemorate this journey with your child. You've never gone through this and hopefully will never experience it again, so it's hard to know what you'll feel like in a week, and you may regret not having the pictures."

The photos weren't a money-grubbing scam—this was a ministry. I thought about it and finally said 'yes'. I was not committing to view or keep the pictures, so we agreed. It was a good decision. It spurred us to track down a friend in the middle of the night, who was a professional photographer, to come and take more pictures.

The firemen, friends, and family all circled me before delivery. They held hands and prayed. They prayed for me, for a miracle....for a crying baby. The nurses said it was time, and a doctor came. Not my doctor, who never showed up. John and my mom, and my sister stayed for the duration. The baby was born. A normal delivery. They gave him to me right away, and he was beautiful.

John kept saying, "He's so perfect, he's so perfect." He did look perfect. John held the baby and me.

Gaetano's lips were strikingly red, and his eyes were closed. His skin was white, but after a time, you could see it would change. He had a little blood in his ears, and I cleaned it out—the only way I could care for him. We took turns holding him for a couple hours. They did all the normal things: weight, measurements. But they gave us a death certificate instead of live birth. Another stab to the heart. And his looks started changing. His lips got redder and redder; his skin peeled.

They took me into another room to heal, but John spent the rest of the night with the baby. He couldn't let go. The professional photographer that came in the middle of the night took more pictures with the family. She took more of the baby and was able to adjust the coloring as he was changing. The pictures were absolutely beautiful, and we used one for the funeral announcement.

They asked if I wanted to join them in the other room, but I was in a different place. The room where they'd put me had Christian music playing. I could literally hear angelic whispers, and I didn't want to miss this peaceful, spiritual part of this experience. I felt assured that Gaetano was okay, that he was in heaven, and that it was beautiful.

John finally had to let the baby go. They wrapped him in a little blue beanie and blanket and put him in the little trolley bassinette. They would keep him and preserve his body there in the hospital until the funeral. When John came over to my room, he was limp, like a puppet with no master to hold him up. He curled next to me in the little hospital bed, but neither of us could sleep, hearing babies cry throughout the night.

> I kept hearing what I figured to be Gaetano's voice, "Mommy, I'm okay. Mommy, I'm with Jesus."

I don't know if my mind was making it up to soothe me or if Jesus was allowing me a glimpse of my baby in heaven to know he was well and alive. John and I both had dreams that night. Our son was playing with blue and red balls. In mine, he was playing handball at school. It was such a whimsical dream. Gaetano climbing trees one minute, flying in heaven the next.

'I'm okay! I'm okay, Mommy!"

I wrote a poem about my dream, and my dad eventually did a painting of it.

We had to stay in the hospital for a while. They had aftercare for us as parents, and they needed to do the investigative work. They did our bloodwork, the baby's blood work, and an autopsy. Everything came back inconclusive at that point. They thought maybe the baby had kicked and fallen on the umbilical cord, but they were guessing. With blood work, they guessed I might have had Antisopholiphic syndrome—a blood clotting issue, but tests always came back negative/positive. But that could mean positive. I think my blood was just thicker. I had placenta previa, but no ruptures, so inconclusive was where we stood.

There was another person left in the dark, as well. Vada had been cared for at home with no idea what had happened. The family felt we were the ones who should tell her, and so my sister-in-law brought her to the hospital unexpectedly. Vada came in, looking around.

"Where's the baby?" she asked.

We scrambled words together, "The baby didn't make it. He's in heaven with Jesus."

She was stunned and started crying. She demanded to see him. By then, he'd had the autopsy and been deceased for many hours. John had a friend at the fire department who worked at the crematory. He was so moved by Vada that he decided to put Gaetano back together and put him in a little casket so that she could see him. They moved Gaetano to a mortuary for Vada's own personal viewing and ceremony. There were candles and music playing—flowers everywhere. We watched her from the doorway, a little apprehensive. The baby looked okay from a distance, but not like the baby we'd held. Vada hadn't seen him before, so she just embraced him and loved him. She sang songs to him, then strode up to us.

"He's beautiful; he's perfect. Go, don't be afraid. Go see him".

And so, we did. But when we saw him, we balked, wondering if this was a joke. Was this really our baby? He looked so different. But Vada was happy and thought he was beautiful. It gave her closure. They kept the viewing open for other family. Soon, it was late, and we realized we had to close the casket. I was sitting on John's lap, just looking at our boy, then folded into my husband, saying I wished I could hold my baby one more time.

I heard my sister-in-law saying, "Here."

I turned to see her holding the baby, offering him into my arms. There were no words to describe the innocence of John's sister at that moment, having scooped the baby from the casket. We feared that this sewn-together baby body could easily fall apart and shock her and Vada to their core. But I gently took him and held him to me so we could all gaze one more time. Then we placed his body in the casket. Although we had confidence that Gaetano was with Jesus for eternity, we couldn't bring ourselves to close the lid. We left that to the mortuary. We bought a little red casket for the funeral and decided we were going to go all out. This was to be all Gaetano's special days wrapped into one: birthdays, graduations, and weddings. It was a ceremony for our little prince.

They kept me in the hospital for three more days. I was still in shock, grieving such a great loss. But it was peaceful as well. Leaving was difficult. I was so well cared for in the hospital; leaving meant walking into a great unknown. There were people to notify, a funeral to plan, and a daughter to explain things to. I was so grateful for all the advice. I was glad to have gone through the birthing process and glad to have the pictures. It could still be my story with Gaetano. It could still be a love story.

I really connected with God and wrote down everything— all the good feelings I had, all the sad feelings I had, all the memories. I have boxes of his love story—journal upon journal and poems. Vada has one baby box. I think Gaetano has five. We even did birthday parties for the first three years. We just felt his nine months of life within me were special and still worth celebrating.

The funeral was full of the colors red and blue, his favorite colors from the dreams John and I had of him. I read my poem, John spoke, the pastor spoke, and my sister-in-law led an altar call. Vada was the front pallbearer. There were little red and blue balls all over the grass in front of the chapel and, of course, the big fire truck. I wish I had hired a videographer to capture every moment. It's my one regret. The advisors in the hospital were so right in their suggestions of experiencing and capturing everything we could of our short time with Gaetano. This was our love story, and I'm so grateful for everything we did to preserve it.

Then the grieving began. I had to go home. Back to our house. Back to the empty beach-themed nursery. With the fire truck and soccer ball. With a closet full of clothes. With the 20 empty pairs of shoes. Gaetano was cremated, and so his ashes were in the house, too.

In hindsight, I would have buried the ashes, so I had a place outside my home to go and grieve. It would be more like an event, a purposeful choice to go and remember him, instead of whizzing by his urn in the rush of daily life. We got necklaces that had little vials of ashes hanging from them. John's was lost in the ocean one day, but it's fitting. We live at the beach, got married at the beach, and now part of Gaetano rests there. We made a memorial in the corner of the house with all the mementos from the service, his bible, the ashes, and pictures, of course. All those things helped me grieve him. It was my place to go to God, to grieve deeply, and have peace that Gaetano was with him in heaven. Eventually, we reduced it. Some visitors wanted to talk about it; others didn't, and the memorial was just too overwhelming to ignore. We wanted this to be about God, the focus on him. So, we reduced everything to just a picture.

We attended a group for parents who had lost babies up to 1 yr, at Hoag Hospital. Some families had attended for over two years, but the sad part was no one knew where their babies were, but we did. We knew that Gaetano was in heaven with Jesus and that their babies were there as well. It was a very depressing and difficult place to be, so we left. Again, in hindsight, I wish I'd stayed to help all those other moms know their babies were in heaven. But our grief was still too raw, and we moved to a grief group at Mariner's Church. This was good for us, looking at death and loss through God's eyes. Soon, we were able to transition to grieving on our own. We read books on grief and read the notes and letters folks had written. Everything helped.

John's grief process was telling his story whenever he could. He had a CPR business, and when teaching the importance of air and breath to live, he shared how his son never took his first breath. I talked only with family and very close friends. This chapter is my first attempt outside my closed circle. I tended to write poems, lots of poems. And letters— 'Dear God' letters asking for help or assurance that my baby was okay.

Every day in my prayer time, I'd say, "I love you, buddy."

And then another miracle came into our life. Six months later, I was pregnant again. We were all so happy but also overly cautious, considering our past experience. I was in the hospital for the last two months of the pregnancy. It was a girl, and she was due Jan 17th, so we moved our Christmas decorations and whole household into my hospital room. We asked the doctor if the baby could be born on Christmas Day, a kind of symbolism of God's promise to us. But the doctor said 'no' that he would be spending Christmas with his family. But on Christmas Day, Vada had just opened her first gift in my hospital room when I started bleeding. They rushed me to surgery and delivered the baby through Caesarean section. Little Italy was placed in my arms....on Christmas Day. God's promise was fulfilled. She was a beautiful, healthy baby girl.

Italy was sooo full of life. Vada and I are introverts, happy with a book or movie. Not Italy. She got us up and moving, and that helped with our healing.

Two years later, I was pregnant again with a boy this time. We struggled with a name. Gaetano was such an important family name to John's dad, but it felt awkward naming this baby Gaetano, as well. We didn't want to diminish our Gaetano in heaven. But the name just started to feel right for this baby. And it was. He was born with the best disposition, and everything he did reminded us of what our Gaetano in heaven would have done at this age or what he might be doing in heaven. Our grieving and healing came to completion with him.

Our first Gaetano never took a breath of air on earth. His first breath was the breath of heaven. What was that like, not having to experience the slings and arrows of this fallen world? What was it like to go from my protective womb to the arms of Jesus? We will ask him one day. Not just us but all who accepted Jesus through his love story. Of this, I am sure.

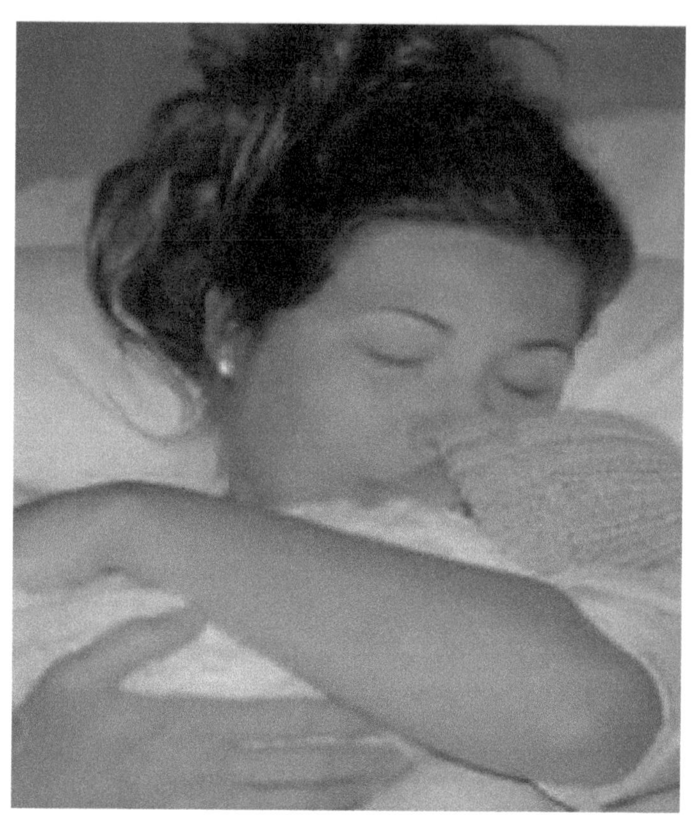

Perla

Fentanyl is an ominous word. The media broadcasts it in connection to the opioid crisis. It sounds nefarious, but it still seems distant until it becomes personal.

My son Daniel Elijah had a heart of gold. He had dreams, big dreams. He wanted to become a businessman with the goal of funding world missions. His desire was to help others who struggled with life on a daily basis and hoped they would come to know the love of God.

Growing up, I was always a believer. I knew Jesus was real, and He loved me, but I was not surrendered to Him. As proof of that, I became pregnant at seventeen—out of wedlock—while still living at home. I was a very young mom in a horrendous home situation. My own parents were both serious addicts. Mother, a crack addict. Father, a heroin addict, and imprisoned for much of my childhood. So, I was the adult in the house.

But Daniel saved my life. Before I got pregnant, my plan to get out of my home was to become a stripper, a Playboy bunny, and an actress and model. I was dazzled by wealth and fame. Instead, I became a single mom for many years—Daniel and I were a team. I went to junior college and took 20 units of parenting classes. I ended up going into social work. I worked as a mental health specialist serving 10+ years for the county of Orange, mostly for OC's healthcare agency. Daniel's father became a middle school math teacher and eventually a professor at John Hopkins University.

When Daniel was four, I separated from his father. It was difficult but necessary. Something wasn't right with him, but I knew I couldn't fix it. I wanted to give Daniel the best possible protection and advantages I didn't have growing up. So, I researched to find the best place to live that I could afford. We moved to Orange County, and I raised him in Los Alamitos, where he attended school and excelled in academics and sports. Growing up, he was so absolute about 'no smoking' and 'no drugs'. "My body is my temple," he would say. He loved basketball, composing music, and singing. Everyone told me what a great kid I had. And he was. He always had his homework done and always had his room clean. He had tons of friends in all social groupings. He was a handsome, smart, considerate, and obedient boy.

I met a man right after I left Daniel's father. He was a soldier, home from Iraq but stationed in Kentucky. He was very sweet and kind, but our dating was long-distance. It took me a year to introduce him to my son, but they hit it off right away. Even though our romantic relationship was on again/off again due to distance and other differences we needed to work out, this strong male role model stayed close to Daniel. As our maturity in life and the Lord grew, I realized this was a good, patient, and loving man. We committed to premarital counseling and abstinence before marriage. We wed six months later. Daniel loved and respected him, always leaving him beautiful cards and letters, especially on Father's Day.

During my son's junior year in high school, I noticed a change in his mood. He seemed withdrawn and appeared to lose interest in everything he once enjoyed. People told me it was the normal teenage rite of passage, but I didn't believe it; the change was too dramatic. His grades plummeted with tardies, and absences followed. He struggled with anxiety and insomnia, and I was at a loss to help him. So, I took Daniel to a psychiatrist. Shortly after, he began regular visits to a therapist. At 17, he was prescribed medication to help with anxiety, insomnia, and depression.

Daniel did not like the idea of taking pills and was concerned with the social stigma that accompanied it. But after a few months, he started to improve, and the doctor suggested taking him off the medication to see how he did. My son was thrilled. However, after a few months, the symptoms returned, worse than ever. But he didn't want to see the therapist again.

> He'd say, "I'm not crazy, Mom. Please stop trying to force this."

He was 18 now, and I could no longer force him to go, but I never stopped encouraging him to seek help.

Daniel continued to struggle and eventually turned to marijuana. He said it helped him sleep. But I couldn't allow this kind of self-medicating behavior in our home and warned him I would know because of the smell.

While competing in track and field, he met kids who were open about taking Xanax. Xanax use was popularized in music and was easily accessible in our neighboring Rossmoor community. Things that were once stigmatized had become popular through the culture and became a youngster's pastime. My son shared with me his thoughts on the practice. He thought Xanax was ok; it mellowed him out, and he wasn't hurting anyone. He thought it was safe because his doctor had prescribed it earlier in his life, and now, he could finally sleep at night.

"It isn't coke or heroine or meth, Mom. It's actually a medication." He didn't see an issue.

But he became addicted. It caught us off guard how fast he became addicted, and we had to put our foot down. He couldn't do drugs in our home. So, he left. I cried out to Jesus that night to protect my son as I'd never cried out before. And God granted me a peaceful sleep. We found out later that Daniel had a near-death experience that night. God had spared my son at the time I had cried out to Him.

Daniel agreed to get help. During this treatment, the therapist found the root cause of his pain. My son revealed that he had been sexually abused by his biological father until the age of five. At the age of nine, Daniel's father relinquished all his parental rights and moved away. By this time, he was a teacher and professor at a distinguished university. I wanted to ruin the man's life—tell his fancy college and send him to prison! But Daniel decided not to confront his father at this time. His goal was to heal and strengthen his relationship with God. I respected his decision but privately hoped justice would be served one day. The depth of Daniel's commitment and faith came on Father's Day. He called his paternal grandma and asked her to call his father and tell him that he loves him and forgives him.

There was peace for a while until Daniel's paternal grandmother got involved. She offered him a place to live with her because she was getting older and needed help. She told Daniel she was scared and lonely. At one point in his addiction, she gave Daniel $700 a month and started taking him to buy drugs when he felt the urge. Daniel's psychiatrist said this was more than enabling; it was hush money. His grandmother didn't want Daniel to reveal that his father (her son) had sexually abused him—it would destroy his career. Daniel had been in recovery up to this point, and grandma was fueling his demise.

We had tried everything to help him heal. We finally turned to Jesus. We talked to Daniel, not our typical Christmas and Easter talk, but the conversation about infusing Jesus into his life. I found a residential Christian immersion program and convinced him to go.

> I told him, "I need to know that if something happens, and you feel the end is near, that you know who to call on and to whom you need to lay down your life. And I need to know you'll be in His kingdom here and forever. What's missing in your life is Jesus." So, we dropped him off.

And Daniel submitted himself, broken before the Lord. He developed a relationship with Jesus, and he was on fire. The plan was for him to be there for a year, but after three months, he left the program. A few months later, refusing to give up on life, my son re-enrolled in the Gooden center, where he completed his treatment program. In July 2020, despite fear of Covid, he found a job and pursued college. He was doing well, and I was so proud of him. We started a schedule of going to church, AA meetings, working, and saving his money. But Grandma begged for him to come to stay with her again. She assured me she had changed.

> A counselor confronted her and told her, "Your actions are killing your grandson. He has a drug tendency and excessive amounts of money, and your enabling is going to end him."

I told her the same thing several times, but she dismissed my opinion. Now, she said she understood and would do her best not to contribute to the problem. We came up with a plan on how best to support him and help him become a responsible adult. She agreed to accept money from each of Daniel's paychecks to teach him to pay bills and save money. It started out ok, but when he tried to give her his earnings to contribute to the household, she refused. That was not part of the plan, and now he had extra spending money.

Daniel started complaining about insomnia again and reached out to his doctor for help. Because of his prior addiction, the doctor was reluctant to prescribe medication and encouraged him to try the holistic approach. He tried exercise, relaxing music, and meditation. Nothing seemed to work.

On Snapchat, he found someone selling Xanax. This dealer was someone a friend recommended and someone my son appeared to trust. On September 15th, my son asked to buy Xanax, but the dealer negotiated a deal on Percocet instead, and my son agreed. The dealer delivered what my son believed was prescription-grade medication. It was not. It was pure Fentanyl, a lethal dose.

That night, I was on the phone with him at 11:00 pm and realized his words were slurred. I thought maybe he'd smoked pot and confronted him.

He denied it, saying, "Why are you always judging me, Mom."

I responded that my judgment was coming from his behavior and slurred speech. Drug use was to be a no-go with his program and with his home life.

I finally said, "You know, Elijah (his middle name but the name I often used), I love you; God bless you." I hung up on him.

He texted back, saying, "I wanna hang. So let's get sleep and call me tomm m I love u an wanna spend time. I miss my momyy."

I could see the words jumbling. I felt burdened for my son, so I went to prayer. And I warred with evil. I asked God to protect my son, to send His angels around him.

When I was done praying, I texted Daniel, "I love you, good night. Angels are there with u."

I've never felt that or said that before. It was truly from God, and I was sure of it at that moment. That was the last thing I said to my son. And the Lord gave me the most peaceful sleep of my life.

My beautiful son died that night.

He had read my last message and began a reply, "let's get coffe and go read our bibles."

He never got to press 'send'. They found him on his knees beside his bed. When I came to the house, I was still so wrapped in the Lord's peace that I could console all the family around. Even his father, who, months before, I wanted to send to prison. The autopsy confirmed drugs and confirmed Fentanyl toxicity. Daniel was deceived, thinking he was taking a legitimate prescription-grade pain pill from someone trustworthy. He ordered 15 pills that night and only took one. The other 14 pills were recovered and tested—all containing a lethal dose of Fentanyl. And this dealer, this young middle-class OC resident, walks free.

Fentanyl seems distant till it becomes personal. And it kills. It killed my son.

I believe Satan used the sexual abuse and my son's feelings of rejection as a gateway to drugs and to gain hold of him. It worked to a point but not into eternity. My son had truly accepted Jesus, and I know he is with Him in heaven.

Now I am left with the aftermath. His father never participated. He made an appearance at the ceremony but never spoke to me. The hardest moment was at the crematorium. I had wanted to take an active part, push the button that sent Daniel's body into eternity. But I lost it. I saw his shaved head where I'd gathered some of his hair to keep. I saw the marks from the autopsy. And I began to wail. Uncontrollably. What I should have remembered was that he was already with Jesus. But letting go of my son's body, for me, was so final—a truly dark night of the soul. Thankfully my husband was there for me. And Jesus— always Jesus. The scripture the Lord gave me during my prayer war for Daniel was really meant for me. Isaiah 54:17 – *"No weapon that is formed against you will succeed."*

The last time I'd seen my son was on my birthday, a week before his death. It was such a wonderful day, sharing a meal; he wrote me a song. While telling me how much he loved me, Daniel inadvertently told me he'd changed all his passcodes to my birthday. This was a huge weapon in the fight ahead of us to bring this drug dealer to justice.

No progress had been made in my son's case. So, armed with my birthday as the passcode, I accessed my son's Snapchat account. Sleuthing through social media, I found and tracked the drug dealer who'd sold my son the counterfeit pills. I saw drug deals go down right before my eyes. I watched a video the dealer posted live. He was heading to buy a car with a designer handbag full of cash. I'm sure all his followers were looking at the cash and the dream car he intended to buy, but I was looking at the background to find his location—CarMax.

There were only two possible locations in the area. I drove to the first, and he wasn't there. But at the second, I saw him making his car deal. I ran in. I was so close to this kid that I could have killed him. This was the monster who had murdered my son. But God had called me to pray for him. Vengeance was not mine.

Detectives had had a hard time finding this dealer to make an arrest. But I did. Here I was, just a mom—an angry, grieving, determined mom—and I found this criminal. The power of one. But I was never a 'one'. I was filled with the Holy Spirit—the very presence of Jesus, and He had guided my path. I called the detective, but he was far from Long Beach. So, I returned to the car where my husband waited and wanted him to return with me and get this kid. My husband said 'no' and prevented me from doing something really risky. God's spirit working in him, as well.

My son's dealer was eventually caught for other crimes, including weapon sales and narcotics charges. While incarcerated, detectives interviewed him. He denied knowing my son and asked for a lawyer. A mere 12 hours after arrest, he was released on bail till his court appearance. But he disappeared and is on the run. I have to trust God that he will eventually get caught again and tried for essentially murdering my son.

Since then, I have filed a civil claim against him for wrongful death. And through my efforts at tracking this criminal, the police were also able to track the big drug distributor. He was arrested by the DEA but only served a few months and has since been released. The DEA has an open case for my son, but no new arrests have been made yet.

Today, I am working with a group of parents that have lost their children to Fentanyl. We have lobbied at the Snapchat headquarters for stricter guidelines. There is much illegal activity on that media. Social media has made it easy to sell and buy drugs.

OC District Attorney Todd Spitzer and several other California DA's have joined our efforts to find 1) A new solution for winning the fight against Fentanyl and 2) Ways to hold Fentanyl dealers accountable for their crimes. Our open borders are surging unfettered with Fentanyl and other deadly drugs. I have shared these thoughts and my testimony in news exposés to law enforcement and elected officials in Sacramento and Washington, DC. In June 2022, I was invited to the first DEA family summit on Fentanyl. They have agreed to support our efforts and asked for our assistance in combating this deadly epidemic.

Fentanyl is personal to me now.

These activities won't bring back my son. But they may save someone else's child. I have regrets of which I need to take ownership. Had I been more sold out to Jesus when I was a new mom and Daniel was young, I might have made better choices with my own life. I shouldn't have gone to clubs and should have lived a godlier life. My biggest regret is having an abortion. If Daniel had had a little brother or sister to bond with, to be an example and protector, he might not have made the choices he did. I don't know that, but it is something I ponder and ask for forgiveness.

I'm still working through the grieving process. It will never end. It's an open wound. But the Lord is allowing scar tissue to form. The scar will help me remember the loss while I move forward in Him together. And I will fight for hope and happiness in this life as I continually hold on to my scripture. It's worth repeating for anyone who needs God's promises to grasp right now.

Isaiah 54:17 –-"*No weapon that is formed against you will succeed.*"

Marci

Not all mothers who lose a child lose them to death. I lost mine to the system.

My husband Bob and I found out early in our marriage that we could not bear biological children. We tried all the therapies, including minor corrective surgery, before we tried Invitro fertilization. After eight years, the doctors couldn't find anything particularly wrong with either of us, but we just couldn't get pregnant. Even the IVF failed. At one point, the cost became too suffocating, especially knowing we wanted to tackle adoption and afford the expenses associated with it.

We finally threw in the IVF flag and sought out information on adoption. The public adoption route was an option, but you had little input or control. And the waiting list was long—so many couples waiting for babies. But Bob and I trusted God. We knew He could fulfill our heart's desire to have children. We knew He had the power and authority to overcome adoption perplexities. And we knew He would give us enough faith in Him to prevail and provide for us.

Someone told us about a private agency, and we liked their approach. We were instructed on how to form a resume as a potential adoptive parent and then given tips on how to get our request into circulation. In a short time, we got a response from a friend of a friend and were contacted by a young woman who wanted to give her baby up. She was an older gal, 34, and I had the exact same birthday as her, so our connection was quick and easy. We agreed to an open adoption which was a new concept at the time. Pictures and updates of the baby would be sent with the possibility of limited visitation now and again. It sounded reasonable to us then, so on September 8, 1985, we were holding baby Sean. It was wonderful—we were drowning in parental bliss.

Everything went smoothly with the mother, who agreed to sign over her rights quickly, but it took several months to get the father to sign. We didn't know how important this step was till the 'Baby Jessica' Deboer case became media fodder. Jessica's birth father had never signed his rights away when the baby was put up for adoption, and he wanted his child. The battle was hard fought by the adoptive parents, but at 2yrs of age, Baby Jessica was removed from the Deboer's loving home and given to the birth father. Thankfully, that didn't happen to us, but we still had to wait on pins and needles till spring, when everything was final. That's a long time to live in fear of losing a child you have come to love with every inch of your life.

We felt very blessed with our situation, so three years later, we began looking for a sibling for Sean. With the help of an adoption lawyer this time, we contacted an organization in San Diego—The Center for Adoption, Youth, and Family Counseling. We agreed to the same parameters for our second adoption since we had had so much success with our first experience. Soon we were paired with a 15 yr. old girl from a very wealthy family on Coronado Island, CA. She was in 9th grade, barely knew her father, and her pregnancy had caused tremendous turmoil in her home. She was kicked out and declared destitute, so all her medical costs were covered by the state. She was fairly far along in her pregnancy, and the father of the child signed away any rights, so the girl was on her own. We went down to meet her, and everything seemed to go well. She had also been adopted and liked us from the get-go.

Soon, we were notified she had chosen us to parent her child. After her decision, we met with her and her parents for dinner, and everyone seemed to be on board. The birth mom and her mom came up to see our home, and we agreed to send pictures and keep her informed. But she just didn't seem that interested. We figured she was closing this chapter in her life. So, on May 25, 1989, Timothy Alexander was born, and we brought him home three days later. We never saw the birth mom in the hospital or after. We sent pictures and messages but nothing.

We were all delighted with our new addition, and Sean was thrilled to have a baby brother and to be a big brother. We did our usual family rounds and visitations, embedding Timmy into the fabric of our family. We were all so content, our lives full, our dreams fulfilled.

In October, about 5 ½ months after absorbing Timmy into our hearts, the birth mom wanted to see us at a park in Dana Point. We were surprised but fine with it, and our meetup seemed to be amicable, other than Timmy was fussy and cried most of the time. But in November, we got a heart-wrenching surprise. Instead of the birth mom relinquishing her rights, she refused to sign off at the last possible hour. She contracted with a lawyer instead, and we soon learned she wanted Timmy back. We were beyond devastated. And we had no idea we were in for the fight of our lives as we entered the legal system again. We were people of faith, and we prayed. At one point, I heard a voice say, "Timmy's yours." Was it God or my own inner thoughts? I don't know, but it gave me peace to soldier on.

A few months later, we had our first hearing with Superior Court, and we won! The judge had considered the length of time we'd had Timmy and our demonstrable love for the child versus the very apparent indifference of the birth mom. He also took into consideration the damaging psychological information in her files. In other words, he kept the best interest of the child foremost in his ruling. We breathed a collective sigh of relief and went home to enjoy our family. But it was not for long...

The birth mom had not filed an appeal, and we were relaxing as we neared the filing cut-off date. But again, at the last minute, she appealed the ruling. We racked up $55,000 in more legal bills (around $550,000 in today's economy) and had to take a second mortgage on our home because Timmy's entire court journey would last almost a year. Timmy was now 15 months old, a bonded and cherished member of our immediate and extended family, and that was priceless.

I was in Kansas visiting family with Timmy and Sean when we heard the appellate court did not rule in our favor. They ruled that the best interest of the child was *not* to be considered when the birth mother wanted the child back in a reasonable amount of time, and they deemed six months reasonable. They failed to realize that the system had stretched it to 15 months, and the child had bonded to a different family, a different mother. It didn't matter. Three days later, we learned that the CA Supreme Court refused to hear the case. In late August, we were ordered to relinquish our child.

I couldn't breathe. We were numb. Nothing seemed real as we gathered up toys, clothes, and belongings that Timmy was so attached to. We knew other families had fled the country, and we were tempted as the dreaded day fell upon us so quickly. But we also knew living on the run was no way to raise Timmy or Sean.

We were scheduled to relinquish him at 6 pm, but the birth mom and her brother showed up 5 hours early. I was at the grocery store buying milk when Bob opened the door to see them standing there. They rushed into the bedroom, grabbed a sleeping Timmy from his crib, and ran out the door and down the street to their car as Timmy screamed his lungs out. They didn't even bother to pick up Timmy's things we'd so lovingly packed for him.

When I came home from the store, I was undone. Tears swirled and fell, and my heart fractured and was unable to contain the enormity of our loss. We didn't even get to kiss Timmy goodbye, so we clung to each other, bracing ourselves for the crushing grief ahead of us. Sean withdrew within himself; actually, physically withdrew to a playroom we'd created for the boys. He couldn't understand the loss of his brother. We went back to work and school, but we were all just going through the motions, somewhat in denial. Would we ever see Timmy again and kiss his smiling face?

I was so angry. Angry at God, at the birth mom, at the system who took us through this long-suffering grueling nightmare. It seemed so senseless. But I learned that God could handle my anger. He never did forsake and pulled us together, keeping our marriage and family strong. But forgiveness was hard. I couldn't understand why we were dredged through all of this. We had faithful hearts and sincere motives. Our pastor would stop by and let us vent and offer words we could hear. Sometimes you must forgive for your own spiritual health because God forgave us and calls us to do the same. Forgiveness is an action, not a feeling; if we're obedient, the forgiving feelings come later.

Within a couple weeks, we received an envelope from the birth mom with all the pictures we sent her of us with Timmy. But Timmy's face had been cut out of every photo. It was overtly cruel but symbolic of the pathetic hole that was left in our lives. We'd been nothing but kind to this young girl, but we also assumed it was evidence of the psychological issues the district court judge had been worried about.

Soon after our loss, we were connected with several other couples that had experienced the loss of their adopted child under very similar circumstances. We met them at the founding meeting of a group called Families for Adoption Reform and Children's Rights. This was a balm on our wound, our saving grace. I was able to grieve with other moms who understood that it is the nurturing that bonds a child to a mother, to a family. They wanted to let the world and the courts know that there is no difference between the bonding of a biological child to his mother and an adoptive child to his mother. The symbiotic relationship between mother and child happens within the first three months of nurturing. Losing a toddler through the court system was exceptionally damaging to the child and adoptive family, and these folks wanted to change the system.

We got heavily involved, a way to funnel and focus our grief. And our efforts were successful. In 1991, the court changed the birth mom's decision window to 91 days. In 2002, it was changed to 30 days, which stands to this day. There was a lot of door-knocking at the Capitol in Sacramento and a lot of pushbacks from birth moms to keep the time extended. But the bonding time and the emotional health of the child was now getting priority, a step in the right direction. Several years later, we were on national TV to highlight the topic. Sarah Purcell of the

Home show and *Maury Povich Show* flew us out for taped interviews.

I'd like to say our grieving was slow but steady, putting our focus on Sean and still entertaining the thought of adding another child to our family. We began looking in Kansas, where the mother only has 72 hours to change her mind about adoption, and we made it crystal clear to any birth mom that we would not go through what we had experienced again.

 But six months after relinquishing Timmy, there was startling news. We got word from our attorney that Timmy was back in the system. He had suffered substantial abuse from the birth mother and birth father. The father had been arrested. Apparently, the pictures were horrific. The birth mom stood by her man, so Timmy was temporarily placed with the grandparents, and she was only allowed monitored visits. We were slayed. How senseless after all this struggle? Our lawyer asked if we wanted to be granted de facto parental status. We agreed. We couldn't turn our backs on Timmy. But soon, we learned that Timmy was caught in a system, and we were far down the line for gaining custody of this poor, bruised, broken child. We didn't know it then, but we would never see Timmy again.

However, God was faithful, and in February of 1992, we were blessed with a daughter from Kansas. And in 72 hours, Breonne was permanently ours. I think Sean struggled a bit, trying to understand why Bre was here—why she stayed, but Timmy was gone. We probably didn't get enough counseling for him or us as we'd muddled through our grief. But eventually, the bond of siblings was formed.

I will never forget Timmy and the love I shared for that beautiful boy. Child loss is child loss. I don't know where he ended up, but I pray he has been placed in a loving environment. I'm also glad for the time we spent marching in Sacramento to change California adoption laws.

But please don't get me wrong. I have the ultimate respect for birth moms. Your nine months of sacrifice do not go unnoticed or unappreciated. Many of you are caught in a tough situation and are forced to make a tougher choice. Maybe knowing there are thousands more adoption applications from women longing and able to raise a baby than there are abortions every year will guide you in your journey to a thoughtful and peaceful decision.

I applaud your love in willingness to give your babies the right to life. I applaud your loving concern in finding the best home for your babies. Not every adoptive family turns out to be ideal. But the reality is, neither do biological ones. Most adoptive families adore the children they are blessed to receive. Losing one, as I did, was like losing a limb—a death to a part of my being. The level of grief revealed the level of love we had for a child considered our own. Remember this when making decisions.

And rely on God. He is loving and forgiving. He will give you His wisdom, His strength, and His grace. Philippians 4:13—"I can do all things in Him who strengthens me."

Suzy

Before I was married, I was sexually active. And I am convinced, now more than ever, that the enemy used that to open the door to more sexual sin. I allowed it, participated, and Satan used it to bring me down — Down to the point of taking the lives of three of my children.

But Christ rescued me.

Baby Michael

I became pregnant while my fiancé was in the Air Force Academy, and he felt obligated to leave and get married. He was able to stay in the service, and soon, my daughter Kim was born. In a couple years, we had Matthew. I was now married with two children when I found myself pregnant with a third child—that was Michael. He was a surprise since I had an IUD for birth control. My husband was still in the Air Force, so we were a military family on a tight budget.

We had not planned on having more children, and my marriage was not stellar due to our youth and shaky start. It was also partially due to my husband's drinking habit acquired during the Vietnam War and partially due to my emotional unfaithfulness.

So, we decided abortion was our solution. A dear Catholic friend knew of my intent and came to me, lovingly encouraging me not to abort our child. But her sincere words did not affect my heart. Abortions were not hard to get, and my heart was cold at knowing what I was actually doing. We had been churchgoers, but neither of us had a relationship with Christ, so I didn't have the Lord in my life to focus on the source of true happiness. I believed my happiness was my husband's responsibility.

My husband went with me to the clinic. The associates there dehumanize the process by telling you that this baby is only tissue and not a living, developing human being. But this procedure, this taking of Michael's life, began a downward spiral within me and within my marriage. We had committed murder, and even though we were hardened to that idea, it was ravaging our innermost being. It affected us spiritually and emotionally in ways we didn't know until later. My heart was so cold that I didn't think I was affected at all by the loss of this baby, and my husband had a vasectomy immediately so as not to repeat this process. Our spiritual lives were dead, and we barely made it to church for Christmas and Easter. If the Holy Spirit was drawing me at this time, I was turning my back.

Baby Michelle

As I continued down the road of not feeling appreciated and my husband not making me happy, I sought approval elsewhere. I became involved with a man at my workplace. I never thought I would be unfaithful in marriage, but I think there's a vibe that one puts out when you're seeking fulfillment. Ironically, I was drawn to someone similar to my husband, which put us in the same social circles. I became friends with his wife, and our kids would periodically play together. The relationship was exciting, it was serious, and we were both betraying our spouses and our families. I was not only hurting my marriage and family, but I was also hurting his.

He was Catholic, so I would go to church with him on Saturdays, so he could go to confession, and then we would go out and sin again. This went on for several months, and then I became pregnant. Since my husband had had a vasectomy, there would be no doubt that I'd been unfaithful if this baby became known. So again, I took the life of my second daughter, Michelle, to save myself and my affair from disaster. There was still no remorse regarding the abortion and the taking of this life, but there was more guilt in the act. Being unfaithful to my husband and hiding the procedure from him made this different from the first time. More lying, more hiding, everything compiling. The father of the child felt responsible and helped to pay for the abortion. He dropped me off at the clinic and picked me up afterward. Everything we did had to be secret, cloaked in darkness, and that made space for raw emotions.

Baby Heidi

But all this trauma and secrecy did not end the affair. Obviously, my relationship with my husband did not improve, and I ended up getting pregnant again. There was no change, no melting of my heart toward taking the life of another precious child. I had this third abortion and continued the affair until my husband was transferred. Our family had to move a long distance away. As far as I knew, my husband never discovered the betrayal—my lies and coverups had become epic at this point. I never wanted him to know or to hurt him and my two living children this way. I was hurting enough for everyone, and I dealt with my pain with sex. However, when you have sex outside of marriage, you take something that is not yours. I was taking fidelity from this man's wife, and he was taking it from my husband. Even when I was young and not married and having premarital sex, I was defrauding a future wife and taking a fidelity that was not mine to take.

Now, I was separated in my heart relationship with my husband, which fueled my marital unhappiness. My husband continued to search for his happiness in a bottle. To cope with this, I got myself to AL-ANON. The talk of a higher power and the presence of many Christians in the group turned my thoughts toward the Lord, and I felt Him pursuing me during that time. My husband was not happy with me going to AL-ANON, and we both started going to counseling together and separately. The counselor felt a family intervention was needed for my husband's drinking. So, we readied ourselves and even set up availability at a rehab facility. Each of the kids wrote a letter to their dad, and I wrote a letter also, expressing our concerns. My husband basically walked out of the session and soon moved out of the house. I was still unfaithful in my marriage even through all this.

My husband and I had both played on an 'over 30s' soccer team when I met Mick, who was also on this team. Our daughters were friends, and that began the conversations. Mick was going through a rough time, struggling with an unfaithful wife. He had hired a private investigator and was hurting knowing the truth. We became friends and started doing fun things together, sharing in each other's lives. But soon, we went from friendship to being sexually active.

When we were both finally divorced, Mick wanted to get married, but he had accepted a job in California for better opportunities as an architect. I told him that I couldn't get married again, I couldn't leave my children, I couldn't leave my job, and I couldn't move to California. But I really did love him. And so, when my son graduated from high school, I married Mick and moved to California.

I had become a member of the Catholic church, so Mick joined the church as well. He had been aligned with the

Anglican church because he knew a bishop personally, but Mick was religious, not necessarily a believer. And we could not get married in the Catholic church unless our previous marriages were annulled, which we were unwilling to do. So, we married in an Anglican church in South Dakota.

We knew of an Anglican priest from South Dakota who had been hired by a church in Southern California, so Mick looked him up and fell in love with the church and the congregation. Something was different there, and we started going to that church. There were bible studies, small groups, and three different styles of worship services, yet one body of believers. We were enthralled and overwhelmed. We both committed our lives to Christ and began a new life in a deepening personal relationship with Him.

I would sit in the front row at church on the far side and weep and weep and weep as the love of Christ was revealed to me, to us. It was good; it was cleansing. We found truth and grace and mercy. We repented of the sins in our past and in our present and found forgiveness like we'd never known before, never knew existed. We were mentored and supported in our new lives with Christ.

As we stepped out into leadership, we were asked to be part of a Discovery of Jesus team. This group would lead a three-day weekend that highlighted 22 small talks from the team that defined life in Christ. One of these weekends, I was given the topic of 'Sin'. And it was time to reveal what I'd left in darkness. In front of all those attendees, I confessed all my sins: my premarital sexuality, marital unfaithfulness, and taking the lives of three children. It was a pivotal moment for me, and my transparency affected many of the lives in attendance.

In the team debrief, something extraordinary happened to me. Satan often attacks the team after these weekends, especially when so many hearts were affected for Christ. This weekend was no different, and I was the prime target. I became overwhelmed with the depth of my sin, the lying, the cheating, and the deaths. I had hurt my first husband and all my children. My living children were struggling with morality in their own lives, and I had to bear some of that burden. I had to take responsibility for relations I'd stolen from other wives. I began to wail and travail as Satan tried to convince me that the three babies I had murdered were in hell and not with Jesus. The gentle arms of a few team members swept me out of the main room and laid hands on me in prayer. Their words and petitions were deep and powerful, and, in the end, any bonds the enemy had left on me were broken. And I was at peace. Perfect peace.

The result of my experience spawned the idea of forming a discreet group for women who had had abortions and were seeking forgiveness. The immediate response was surprising, even from men who had participated in paying for or encouraging the abortion of their child.

I became part of an intimate group of six women. The participants had come to realize that abortion was murder, and their suffering was great. Some women had had abortions more recently than others. Some had had one many years ago, and the effect was now reaching its full measure. Just like me, they had been told and were convinced that abortion was their right, that it was safe, and that the baby was just a clump of cells. Ironically, we are all just a clump of cells. The hearts of these precious women had been hardened to the truth, but Christ was breaking down the wall, entering, softening. Christ empowered me and my co-leader to help these tender souls find the peace and forgiveness they yearned for, the bounty we had received.

Ezekiel 11:19 – "And I will give them one heart, and a new spirit I will put within them. I will remove the heart of stone from their body and give them a heart of flesh."

The need for these groups has continued. The ability to reach suffering women has been challenging due to the desire for secrecy and confidentiality. Often shame or fear of repercussions in an immoral world that would condemn their regret are barriers to connecting. But time and messaging have improved, and there are now many groups for post-abortive women and men who have advocated for abortions. Linda Cochrane's two books, *Forgiven and Set Free* and *Healing a Father's Heart*, have been instrumental in the journey to forgiveness and peace.

Christ rescued me. He is the difference. He changes everything. Jesus gives us a heart of flesh, and when that exposes the depth of our sin, He forgives us and gives us a peace that passes all understanding. We cannot find that kind of peace anywhere else. It is worth your commitment, worth your life. And it can save the lives of many others, some of the most vulnerable, who need us to love and protect them.

I carry scars and endure consequences. I do not have any grandchildren. My son still suffers with his identity in Christ, and I bear responsibility for that. My daughter also struggled but has found her way to Christ and back to me. She is my most precious friend these days, and we are making up for a lost time, delighting in the Lord's promise in Joel 2:25 – "I will restore to you the years that the swarming locust have eaten." Together we pray and reach out to my son.

I know I will meet Michael, Michelle, and Heidi in heaven. For now, they are in the loving care of the Savior, the best possible place they could be. My Mick is with them as well, lost to me from cancer. But God has blessed me with a December marriage. Life is beautiful in Christ. He is the difference. He is our all in all.

Author A.R. Torres made this observation on life…

> "That is how life is, it gives us burdens to carry and doesn't give a damn about the weight. We shoulder it, or we break."

That is not true in a life in Christ…

Matthew 11:28-30 – "Come to me, all who labor and are heavy laden, and I will give you rest. Take my yoke upon you, and learn from me, for I am gentle and lowly in heart, and you will find rest for your souls. For my yoke is easy, and my burden is light."

Susan

I remember holding you in my arms, so tiny, so helpless; all curled up in a fetal position.

Lydia Rose, you took my breath away.

Born into a family that loved you more than words, soon your nickname would become Itty Bitty Liddy. As I cried and prayed over you, I knew I had to trust God's plan for your life and believe you would grow up to do great and mighty things, even though you were born the smallest of our daughters. Ultimately, *my* faith would be tested as the weight of life became too heavy for you to carry.

Along with your two sisters, Lindsey and Hannah, you had the destiny to know and love God. You had the blessing of being raised in a spirit-filled home surrounded by the beautiful nature God created. Your dad and I wanted you girls to be protected from a concrete world and be free to explore South Florida's tropical paradise.

One month after your birth, you were dedicated to the Lord. We knew you were only on loan to us, and we vowed, along with our spiritual community, to raise you knowing His fullness. At age four, you accepted Jesus as your Lord and Savior. It was one of those pivotal moments of joy I longed for as your mom—your name written in the Lamb's Book of Life.

One evening, around age five, we lay on our trampoline looking up at the stars. "Momma, do you see that man in the sky?" I kept silent, hoping for her explanation, my head focused on the nursery rhyme. "Do you know why there is a man on the moon, Momma? That man is Jesus because

He is the light in the darkness." Again, this young one took my breath away. God had given Lydia the gift of intuition. She already saw the deep truths of God.

Lydia grew to know who Jesus was, whose she was and that her life was not her own. Lydia made sure all those close to her knew that too. At the age of seven, she even led her best friend's mom—my best friend—to the Lord. Because of Lydia's boldness, my friend lives forever in heaven. Oh, the joy of seeing your child unashamed and unafraid, telling others about Jesus. At nine, she was baptized on Miami Beach, along with her sister Hannah. Our friends and extended family watched, agreeing to support us, as she publicly acknowledged that she would serve God for the rest of her days. It was a day we would never forget. I don't think we knew how important that support system would become for us.

But in middle school, we noticed a change. Lydia had always been very advanced in school, which also created a social circle of much older kids. Things were introduced to her too early, and though we did our best to keep her grounded, the pressures from peers influenced her in a very negative way. We tried to be proactive but discovered she was experimenting with different drugs and cutting herself. There were counselors, rehabs, and court appearances. We knew if we didn't have a professional intervention, we might lose her.

One afternoon, Lydia didn't come home from school. Where was my child?! The weight of that suffocated me. I called everyone I knew. I called all her friends. I called the school. I drove up and down streets, but she was nowhere to be found. Night after night, we cried ourselves to sleep. This was the straw that broke us.

My husband, Barry, and I decided to petition the courts for aid in locating Lydia as we felt she was a danger to herself. Days later, we received the call we so desperately wanted to hear.

"We found your daughter." And then, the part we dreaded.
"Can you come to the ER as soon as possible?"

We frantically asked questions, but they wouldn't answer. To me, this was debilitating. Where had she been? What had she done? Lord, help us! As her dad and I sped for 40 miles, there were tears, prayers, and that feeling of hopelessness. The whole drive we wondered if she was still alive or dead. Once we arrived in the ER, we were informed that Lydia had been living at a friend's house and had overdosed on cheap cough medicine. We entered the room and saw her covered in black residue from having her stomach pumped. She was alive. But now, what do we do? We didn't understand this rebellion. After all, she was raised to make good choices, raised to know the Lord, and she had given her life to serving Him. All three of our girls were raised the same, in a godly home, by godly parents surrounded by godly friends. I was a stay-at-home mom and loved it—family was my world. But somehow, hell was getting a foothold, and we were undone.

We decided to have authorities take her to a mental health center where professionals could help us find the root cause of this chaos, but it remained a mystery. Though we truly didn't understand, God's 'peace that passeth all understanding' was ours through the valley. And the scripture that guided these dark times was Proverbs 22:6, *"Train up a child in the way they should go and when they are old, they will not depart"*...wait what??? **When they are OLD?** Not when they are teenagers?!

As a dedicated follower of Jesus, in ministry for over 30 years, I had this false sense of security. I thought I would have a free ride from experiencing parenting disappointments. I couldn't have been farther from the truth. The picture I had created of that perfect family would be tested beyond my comprehension. I began to doubt myself as a parent, as a mother, and as a Christian. Questions swirled in my mind: Had I done enough? Did I need to do more? Had I favored one child over the other? Soon those thoughts would haunt my very existence.

Lydia chose not to go to college after high school. We told her she could live at home, but she'd need to work, and we required one night of 'forced family fun'. She reluctantly agreed. She never wanted to be a burden and insisted she would provide her extras. Lydia worked two jobs—one at a local veterinarian clinic. She loved animals, was always compassionate for the underdog and brought abandoned dogs home to nurture them back to health. One, named Faby, would become her lifelong companion.

The following year, our middle daughter Hannah married and moved out. Our oldest, Lindsey, and her husband, Jason, convinced Lydia to move to Tennessee and attend trade school. Lindsey was a phlebotomist and felt certain that if Lydia could complete her schooling, she could get a job. Lydia agreed, so we became empty nesters. Although I would always be known as a mom, the daily activities of *being* a mom had changed forever. I felt my purpose was over.

It wasn't long until Lydia graduated from trade school, found a great job, and got her own apartment. She re-dedicated her life to Christ, realizing she needed Him more than ever. We loved seeing her walk in the purposes and plans God had ordained for her. But soon, that would all be challenged...again. Behavioral changes escalated. Lydia lost her job and moved to a different apartment. She withdrew. She wouldn't answer the door when the family came over. The time between calls/texts was extensive. Eventually, we would get a text, "Everything's fine." But she wasn't fine.

We heard hints that some distant family members suffered from mental illnesses: anxiety, depression, and even schizophrenia. But it never crossed our minds that Lydia was heading into the ravages of mental illness, even with the dark time in her teens. As a mom, what do you do? My husband and I counseled our doctor. We spoke to pastors. We had an extensive intercessory prayer team that prayed, believing Lydia would be okay. We trusted God to make everything right. Isn't that what He does for every believer? His word says, *"All things work together for good to those called according to His purpose."* Romans 8:28.

I went to Tennessee to discern, as Mom, if any drug use or unhealthy relationships were to blame. I found Lydia, not the same child I raised. She was not the happy-go-lucky, funny, and helpful person she was when she left home. So, we made the tough decision to convince Lydia to move back home. My husband had had major back surgery, and we really needed help. We felt if we could just get her back home, we could watch for warning signs.

I think the hardest thing a mom experiences is seeing her child struggle and not being able to fix them. In fact, there were unfathomable moments that destroyed my thought processes and chipped away at my faith. Had we missed the mark? I thought she had had victory over those strongholds. Had we not prayed over her enough? Oh God, help our unbelief.

Although we knew that God was on our side, we still had to deal with things in the physical realm. We understood we were not wrestling against flesh and blood but...against the spiritual forces of evil. Ephesians 6:12. But Mama Bears go to battle when seeing their child suffer. We finally convinced Lydia to see our physician to check her for disease or hormonal imbalance. After thousands of dollars of testing, nothing but excessive weight gain was alarming. Now, we knew mental health care was needed. But she refused. And she was an adult.

Having Lydia move home felt right, but it was not easy. She was regressing and became disconnected, isolating herself in her room and locking her dog in the kennel. Her mind became consumed with paranoia. She was constantly on edge—from extreme anger to extreme happiness. I struggled daily with not knowing what to do. We discussed professional help, but she always declined, dismissing our thoughts on mental illness.

Some may question if I was mad at God. I honestly have to say, no, I wasn't. Did I feel lost and confused? Of course. Did I think God wasn't listening to our hearts cry puddles of tears? Absolutely. But I never got angry *at* God.

After a difficult divorce, our daughter, Hannah, moved home, needing help raising her 2yr old, Eliana. Our home resounded with joy and laughter again. But we were constantly on edge, buffering our granddaughter from Lydia's rage or her manic outbursts of laughter. Or...Lydia's conversations with someone who wasn't there.

Some days Lydia would visit me in my pottery studio or join me in the kitchen to cook. I loved those moments having her nearby. But she was short-tempered and easily frustrated if something wasn't good enough. If you asked a question, she would get angry as if her character was in question.

My husband was up most nights with chronic back pain, and Lydia was a night owl. So, this became daddy-daughter time. There was something special about their relationship. I loved it, yet I felt left out. 'Mom' conversations seemed so trivial. But in those late-night hours, dad had to deal with her unrealistic views and conspiracy theories. He had to bring her mind back to reality which often ended in teary breakdowns. In those dark nights and lonely days, Lydia was struggling to live.

Several mornings just after Thanksgiving, she came out of her room and sat beside me. She'd been crying, and I turned to her.

"Whatever's bothering you, we can work through it together," I said.

I tapped the boxing glove charm she wore every day—a graduation gift from me. It was a reminder that I'd always fight in her corner when life got too hard. But all she did now was shake her head and cry. In hindsight, I think she knew her time on earth was ending.

With Christmas only a few weeks away, I prepared our family craft tradition. Each year since the kids were born, they decorated a new handmade ornament. This was so that when my girls left home, they would have memories of decorating their own Christmas trees. This year, I created little wooden sleds to paint in their favorite colors. We'd barely started when Lydia became frustrated, took her brush, and aggressively swirled all her paints together. Red, silver, and black were now a dark muddled mess. Our 6yr old granddaughter was confused with no filter.

"Why did you do that? Are you crazy? What's wrong?
That's ugly!"

I held my breath. I knew Eliana didn't mean it the way it
sounded. She was just speaking from a young mind. But it
triggered Lydia, who immediately rushed to her room and
locked the door. Flashbacks of middle school surfaced, and
I felt helpless. I tried to bury my fears while reassuring
Eliana, but inside I was crying out to God. I cried and
prayed, then cried some more. How could these happy
moments become so sad so quickly? This had gone on long
enough. We had to convince Lydia that she didn't have to
live like this. There was help, and we could get it for her.
She was in a very dark place, and I hoped we hadn't waited
too long to intervene. But now she was 27. Both sisters
tried to talk to her, but she ignored them. Our
granddaughter would take her dolls and ask her to play,
but she refused. After these intense outbursts over the
past several months, we knew it was time for intense
intervention. But I thought, if I could just get through
Christmas and to the first of the year, maybe...just maybe,
things would be better.

Finally, it was Christmas Eve, and we all dressed in
matching jammies for family photos. Hannah had to work
and wouldn't be home to open gifts Christmas morning, so
she and Eliana opened their gifts that night. But after they
opened gifts, Lydia went into the laundry room and came
out in casual clothes. Odd at 10 pm, but I shrugged it off.
Maybe she didn't like the color of the jammies, or maybe
they didn't fit her right. It was obvious she wasn't happy.
How could I help?

"I'm going to bed now, Lydia. See you early in the
morning."

I made eye contact as she leaned her cheek to get a kiss goodnight. She'd grown affectionately detached, yet she let me kiss her cheek, then she turned and walked away.

Sometime after midnight, my husband came into the bedroom and shook me awake.

> "Something's wrong. She's gone!" Still groggy, I couldn't comprehend. He reiterated, "Lydia's gone! Her car is gone. I was dozing off but heard her rummaging in her room. Out of the corner of my eye, I saw her walking past with her dog. I thought she was taking Faby out to go potty. She paused as if she was going to say something to me, but she never looked back."

At that moment, my peace was challenged again. Where had she gone? Was it something I'd said? Was there something we could have done to keep her home? Did having her dress up with us cause anxiety? Did she hate that she didn't have a job or money to buy us gifts? My mind was racing to every scenario possible. Did she have a verbal altercation with her sisters? Did Eliana want her to play too much? Did her dog require too much attention? I had plenty of questions but no answers.

After numerous texts and calls with no response, I asked my husband what he wanted to do. It wasn't uncommon for Lydia to take day trips with her dog; she always came back. But this was Christmas Day. The silence caused great concern. She knew this was the most important season of all to me. How could she disrespect me that way? How could she interrupt *my* plans? We finally decided if she wasn't home by noon, we would call the police.

Around 8 am, Eliana woke up bright-eyed, excited to open gifts. We Facetimed our Tennessee kids to open gifts together, but there was an oppressive atmosphere present. The unknown was terrifying. Later that day, we called the police. Something just didn't seem right, yet it seemed all too familiar. Just like our feelings during her teen runaway episode. Oh God, how we need you like never before. That peace that surpassed all understanding seemed nowhere to be found.

Monday—still no answer to calls or texts. By 8 am, I had to get myself together as I was a private caregiver to an elderly couple. Around 10 am, I got a text from my husband asking for photos of Lydia. I was confused since we'd already given detectives photos when filing the missing person report. About 45 min later, I received another text. 'Come home.' I couldn't breathe.

When I arrived home, there were two police cars and a homicide detective van. At that moment, I realized my baby was gone. Forever.

The joys of Christmas day would never be the same.

My husband tried desperately to console me, but disbelief, anger, and frustration came out in screaming sobs. I asked the detective to tell me where she was, but he refused to give me any details as it was a crime scene. I was so angry. I beat the top of my car to get his attention.

"I'm her mother, and I need to hold her!"

Could she still be alive? Was she really dead? Where was her dog? In the pit of my stomach, I knew, but my eyes had to see. I'm very visual, much like doubting Thomas, I suppose.

On Christmas day 2016, Lydia took the life of her fur baby, Faby, then shot herself.

Why??? Why her pup? Why Christmas day? Why??? Why??? This was our family's favorite holiday. This was a time we celebrated the birth of our Lord. Where was the note to explain this senseless and permanent decision? Did she truly think she was a burden? Could we have talked her out of this? What triggered her? Was I not grateful enough for the dessert she made last night? Was there something my husband could have asked her as she walked out on Christmas Day? Did she think about never coming back home as she drove away? Was she hungry? Did she still love us? Wasn't our love enough for her? How could she have done this? Would any of these questions ever be answered on this side of heaven? Even giving Lydia the best home life possible and assuring her she was loved and accepted didn't stop the pain she lived with 24/7. Why would God allow someone not in their right mind so much suffering? How do I live one more day without my baby girl? I was suffocating.

So now what? She had to be cremated as it had been too long from the time of death to discovery. How do I do this? How do we move forward with funeral plans? It shouldn't be like this. Parents aren't supposed to bury their children. It's much too soon. How do we face tomorrow? But we had to bring closure, not only for us but for all who loved her.

Years ago, Lydia had babysat for close friends whose daughter had become a mortician. She kindly walked us through and even made arrangements for me to be present at the cremation. I had to be there. I brought her into this world and vowed to be with her to the bitter end. I just imagined it would be my end, not hers.

On Jan 1, we held Lydia's home-going service—a remembrance of her life, not her death. It was an opportunity for us to honor her and tell of all the wonderful things she had done. To honor Lydia, we passed out stones for guests to take home or to give the stone away as they shared her story. At the end of the service, our pastor presented us with a beautiful painting from a prophetic artist that was completed during the Christmas Eve service we had missed. In it was an angel carrying a red heart. It was exactly what I needed—a visual reminder that the Lord had taken Lydia out from the darkness of her world and called her to heaven. She would never be okay on earth, and He knew that. Suddenly, we could see a bit clearer.

Many shared their condolences, but two people impacted my life forever. The first was a very close friend. She looked me in the eyes and said,

"All Lydia's questions have now been answered!"

The memory still runs down my cheek. That very instant, not only did I know where Lydia was, but I knew she was safe. God met her the moment that gun was fired, and I didn't have to worry about her tormented mind anymore. I was weak in the knees as we hugged and cried. Some think suicide is an unforgivable sin because you die before you've asked for forgiveness. Not true. Jesus died for your sins—past, present, and future. If you are His, you are His for eternity, Romans 8:38-39.

Near the end of the 2-hour condolence line stood a lady I recognized though we'd never spoken. Five years prior, her adult daughter had died of suicide. I'd heard her story from conversations at the pottery league where we had our 'forced family fun'. I knew at that moment that I wasn't alone. No words exchanged. Just a smile and a nod to say, 'I understand'. It was so profound. So many friends tried to find the right words, but no one could say anything that helped. They meant well, but the silent strength of a fellow grieving mom was just what I needed. After that night, we developed a friendship much deeper than words. And soon, we found there were more of us.

The goodbyes were over, and people went back to their normal lives. All our kids left for Tennessee to give Barry and me time to grieve, while sisters took the opportunity to restore their relationship. It was time for us to face all that was lost. My days were consumed trying to wrap my mind around this suffocating sorrow. I cried uncontrollably at the thought of never seeing my daughter again. Total breakdowns descended while trying to accomplish one task a day. Where could I find answers? What did I miss? I continued to search for clues, so desperately wanting to know if Lydia had thought of me prior to her death. But slowly, a realization came.

Lydia's death wasn't about me or anyone else. Her distorted thought process focused on *her* and the searing pain *she* endured from carrying the weight of the world.

Two months later, finally having the courage to put away Christmas decorations, I found more insights. My husband had noticed Lydia intensely looking at the tree several nights before Christmas. He thought she was just rearranging the ornaments. And, in fact, she was. As I began to remove ornaments...there, next to my sled, was hers. Tucked in my sled was a money order I'd given her on her birthday. At the bottom, I'd written, "I will always love you." She *had* thought of me; this was her way. As we explored, we realized she had thought of everyone. She gave my husband an unusual gift just before Christmas. She emailed one of her sisters, telling her where her necklace was. She gave a few dollars to her niece to buy candy.

Later we found clues that shed light on her decision to leave this earth. She had cleaned her car, destroyed all her identification, and given away personal items. *Oh, Lydia, if we only knew the depth of your pain, the struggle to exist just one more day. Now we do, and we will not be silent.*

The months after Lydia's passing were a complete blur. It was so difficult to do much of anything. I didn't want to clean the house. I didn't go to church. We avoided many of our friends and activities. We communicated by text and face timed our kids but mostly stayed to ourselves. The suffocating sorrow was overwhelming. There were days I couldn't do anything but shake my head in unbelief. There were days filled with so much anger. And days, I just cried continuously. I never thought I'd find happiness again. Yet, somehow, I still trusted God.

Two months after losing Lydia, a friend asked me what she could do for neighbors that had lost an adult child to suicide. Seriously? How was I to comfort anyone when I was experiencing such anguish? My supportive husband didn't understand a mother's loss. How could he? He had his own grief to manage. My children couldn't comprehend my pain, nor my pastors, nor family, nor friends. But I couldn't allow another mom to walk this road alone, so we met. It was a safe place to share our unique pain of suicide loss—to shed tears and tell stories of our children without guilt or condemnation. Soon, another mom contacted me. Then another. We became members of a club that no one asked to join.

Our group of Angel moms found creative ways to leave words of hope around town, bringing awareness to the silence of suicide. We also longed for a communal way to heal, allowing God to mend our broken hearts. A bible study was suggested, and it was transformative. Now no other mother would have to live her reality alone. Tragedy brought us together, but our deep love for one another kept our sisterhood strong and kept memories of our lost alive.

I read somewhere that you will live with grief for the rest of your life because grief was an outward expression of just how much you love somebody. So, when I actually woke up with a smile one morning, guilt began to overwhelm me. But the Holy Spirit speaks to me in pictures, and He gave me a vivid one—a timeline of my life: **12-25-2016 = Suffocating Sorrow…….6 months ~ Grief Begins……Heaven ~ Fullness of Joy**

Each day that passed from Lydia's death till I get to heaven meant I was further away from suffocating sorrow and one day closer to the fullness of joy. Everyone has a different timeline, but this was mine. Psalm 30:5 became so clear to me, *"Weeping may endure for a night, but joy comes in the morning."* It doesn't mean a 24-hour day. I had wept for six months, and now I was grieving. There is a difference. Until my last breath on earth, I will grieve because of my deep love for Lydia, yet God is allowing me happiness as well. Every day closer to heaven means I will be just a little bit happier. This divine revelation explained why I was happy and that it was okay. I could choose joy, or I could choose sorrow. I chose Jesus.

It was now the month before Christmas 2017, and we faced the first anniversary. The day that ripped our hearts apart. Anniversaries should mark happy times, but we did not want to face this day. Christmas was always our favorite time of year, but my husband decided he didn't want to celebrate Christmas again. He was adamant—no decorations, nothing. I honored his request. Difficult, but I understood.

More difficult was explaining to our granddaughter that we were just too sad with Lydia gone and we would not join in on the celebration. Our tender-hearted Eliana pleaded, "But Nana, I'm still here." I realized at that moment we still had to share the true reason for the season. It was important to keep things somehow normal for Eliana and our family. One thing hadn't changed—God was still good. His word promised me He would never leave me nor forsake me. The Lord would have to help me through. Christmas was never going to be the same, and that was okay. We found a way to replace the old and sad with happy and new. The first year, I took the money we would have spent on gifts for Lydia and chose a single mother that was struggling. The next year, I donated blood that would help save the lives of three others. Somehow this made the season more meaningful. I had too much love to throw it all away. We still find different ways to celebrate Lydia. Sometimes, we pay for someone's cake at a bakery on her birthday because I'm missing my Lydia Rose. And until my last breath, there will be a new ornament for her every Christmas.

So, what has changed me forever?

~I am more aware than ever that believer or non-believer, mental illness exists. Mental illness is no respecter of person, place, creed or color, career status, or financial acumen.

~I am more aware than ever that mental illness is a silent killer—that many people say they're ok, but they're not.
~I am more aware than ever that what this world needs is Jesus, for without Him, there is no hope, and there is no peace. Do you know this Jesus?
~I am more aware than ever that with Jesus and my life-changing awareness, I will not be silent!
The loss of Lydia will always be marred by sadness. But I know one day, I will see that sweet face again. And I will choose the joy of knowing that each day she is gone from us, she is in the presence of Jesus.
~And I'm more aware than ever..... He takes her breath away.

Judy

I don't know why I cried for so many years. Eight years I cried. I understand that tears are important for a season, but not to the level I carried it. Sam left us at the peak of his life, just 39 years old. He wasn't a child, but he was *my* child. He had a great marriage to Kristy and loved being a dad to Sam Jr. (Sammy) and Blair. We were so close. The whole of his life, he and I were so connected.

Kristy didn't cook, so Sam was the chef in the family, and he was always calling me for recipes. He cooked everything, including the Thanksgiving turkeys. I was so proud of the husband and father he'd become. His marriage was a good balance—Kristy was as organized as Sam was freewheeling. She kept order, and he made it fun. They were such a great match. Sam was such a good, good man.

Sam had always had a goodness about him, even as a little guy. He was the 4th and last child, the 3rd boy. My oldest was Linda, the typical oldest child—well-behaved and an achiever. But next came twin boys, Tyler and Taylor. And they unraveled me. The doctor said he'd never seen kids this hyper. And that was at six months. With these two little dickens having ADHD off the charts, my hands were full. I felt very alone during that season. I was always the object of their nasty words and their wrath.

My husband was a good provider but preferred directing me on how to manage the kids instead of him doing it directly. Since Linda was always daddy's girl, I had no one in my court to carry the load with these very difficult kids, who had no love-loss toward me. I felt helpless, worthless...unloved.

Then along came Sam, my hero child, my protector. He was just so dang cute. He was always happy and would always temper the twins, telling them to knock it off and give mom a break. When the twins were teens, and I was 'the bitch', Sam was my hope, my reason to keep persevering as a mom. He was always so proud to show me off. There was no jealousy among siblings because the rest of the family adored Sam, too. It was hard to have animosity with his winsome personality. He was never mean and always had a sense of fairness. He was our Super Sam. Everywhere he went, he had lots of male friends and lots of girlfriends—such a magnetism about him.

He was willing to hug his guy friends and say," I love ya, man!" Not typical in an East coaster.

Sam graduated from a small college, but he was led to sales. This did not please Kristy's parents, as she was a Yale grad and a scientist. But with Sam's personality, he soared in sales. He started in select product sales but went to gourmet foods, then sales to the major grocery chains. Kristy's parents were reticent to give a salesman their blessing to marry their Ivy League daughter, but they finally came around. Just like everyone else came around to Sam, he was the social glue that made relationships happen and kept them together.

After seven years, Sam and Kristy, Sammy Jr., and Blair took a trip up to Maine to visit my sister. They enjoyed a lot of raw oysters up there, so when Sam started experiencing digestive pains, they attributed it to the shellfish. He couldn't eat. He had blisters in his mouth. He became extremely careful about what he would put in his mouth.

After many extensive tests, Sam was diagnosed with Crohn's Disease at Yale New Haven Hospital and was put on an infused medication. He was on that for 6-10 months but still felt cruddy. They switched to another medication, but that didn't work either. His mouth hurt all the time, and he had a hard time swallowing. He'd gone from 220 lbs. in August to 180 lbs. in November. Our research on Crohn's mentioned nothing about painful spots in the throat, like thrush. So, on went the mystery. Sam took Prednisone so he could eat and probably took more than prescribed because he really wanted to get feeling better. He developed 'sweet syndrome' where his whole body was covered with pimples—a side effect from one of the Crohn's medications.

Despite all the uncomfortableness and pain, Sam powered through. He did all the dad things; he did all the husband things; he kept trying to be the good man that he wanted to be. And he was.

In January, he called me after work and complained about his painful throat in a rusty voice. I implored him to see his doctor. The next day he and Kristy went to his GI doctor. The Doc thought it was just a cold and prescribed a Z-Pac. The next day they were getting their carpets cleaned, so Sam stayed home from work to advise the cleaners and deal with his sore throat. He watched TV, mentioned his throat to Kristy when she came home, and then went upstairs to lie down.

When she checked on him later, Sam was unresponsive. She called a neighbor who was a paramedic. When he checked Sam, he had coded, and our neighbor called 911. The paramedic friend worked on Sam, got him breathing, and rode with him to the hospital. Dad and I were notified, and we streaked to the hospital. By then, they said Sam had died again for almost 8 min, but they'd brought him back. My obvious worry was brain damage. They said he'd been hooked up with oxygen, so they weren't worried about that. But Sam was still unconscious, so we stayed the night there in the hospital while Sam remained in the ER in ICU.

By that evening, he was spurting rectal blood, and that's when doctors hinted that we should be prepared. Till then, I had no clue that Sam would die. I just did not believe he was going to die. But apparently, he was septic and had been since the night before. I was clueless.

The next morning was Saturday, and his paramedic friend stopped by on his way to work, wanting to see Sam. He went straight to the ICU and was told by the staff that Sam was not going to make it. We had not been told this yet, so it was extremely hard for this friend to be the one to come tell us. This was his good buddy's wife and parents, and he was consigned to tell Sam's own flesh and blood that he was not going to live.

Sam never regained consciousness. Kristy's parents drove up with the kids so they could say goodbye. We all gathered around Sam and assured him that 'we've got this'. We assured him we'd take care of his wife and kids. He could go peacefully. And so, he did. At 8:00 am in the morning..... our Super Sam was gone.

His cause of death was listed as Crohn's, and with shift changes and paperwork on the weekend, the staff didn't put in for an autopsy. I was livid. What brought him to the hospital was a raging sore throat which was supposedly unrelated to Crohn's. We had to really push for an autopsy. The pulmonary doctor and the doctor from Yale New

Haven Hospital were still there. They said the family could pay for an autopsy, and that's when I fought back.

"Do you think it's right for a 35yr old newly widowed wife to pay for an autopsy?! There are obvious mysteries here that need to be understood."

So, the Yale doctor put in a special request, and they autopsied the throat only. And nothing was there. After that discovery, they opened the thoracic cavity and stomach area. He called us to report that there were no signs of Crohn's. This was very odd. Your colon gets scarred and pebbled with Crohn's, and there was nothing like that in Sam at all. He was septic, but the cause unknown.

The doctor did feel that if Sam had come into the hospital after work on Friday, he would have made it. The doc felt that they could have controlled the sepsis, which they proposed came from the sore throat. But the sore throat and stomach issues remained somewhat a mystery. My GI doc said Yale New Haven rarely makes mistakes. But he also said Crohn's patients rarely die from Crohn's. So, my strong, vibrant 39yr old was taken down in his prime cause unknown.

Sam was always glad I prayed, but faith wasn't important to him. For most of Sam's life, we were devout Catholics. But Kristy was non-religious, so they decided to let the kids make their own decisions about faith because, again, religion wasn't important to them. As Sam was dying, one of the twins prompted us to call a priest. We did, and one came to administer Last Rites. With no commitment to a Catholic church or any church, there were questions about where Sam could be buried. Fortunately, having received Last Rites made Catholic burial possible. We had a friend who was a priest in New Haven, and he paved the way for a service at St. Mary's with burial in St. Lawrence Cemetery near where Sam and Kristy lived.

I never thought I would bury a child. Never. Especially not my youngest child. Especially not *this* blessed child. My husband and our son Tyler made all the plans for the funeral and paid for it. They did the hard parts. I couldn't...I just couldn't. They would okay things with Kristy and me at times, but I was a basket case. When we were at the funeral home, I asked Kristy's father if he would go help her pick out a suit to bury Steve in. I couldn't do it. But he said 'nope'. They'd bury him in his Patriot shirt, his cargo shorts, and flip-flops. I think I smiled for the first time in a week. They also tucked in a container of ashes from his favorite dog, Brady. And they put in a joint, which brought a chuckle from everyone.

The rest of the process was such a painful time. The funeral was an awful experience, an awful, awful experience. I always had a strong faith in God, but this seemed just too big to handle. People were so supportive of us. Many could hardly speak Sam's name without crying. The funeral was absolutely packed, standing room only. Sam's work headquarters flew their flag at half-mast and allowed most employees time off to attend his service. Friends from high school, college, and work attended. Eight guys at his funeral called Sam their best friend.

Sam's college roommate, John, was supposed to get married, and Sam was to be his best man. He didn't know how he could do it without Sam being there. Later that year, Taylor, one of our twins, would go and stand in for Sam at John's wedding. So, you see, despite all the twin's early struggles with ADHD, they did grow up to be fine, honorable men.

People were so loving and so supportive to Kristy and the kids at the funeral. There were so many promises made that these friends would be there for the kids, to help them grow up. But not one of them actually followed through. Not a frickin' one. That was one of my biggest disappointments. I saw this great 7yr. old boy and darling 4yr. old girl lose a fantastic dad, the greatest man in their life, and they were slowly abandoned. I found out later that some did try to include Sammy and Blair, but Kristy was resistant, and eventually, they just stopped trying. She was grieving her own way. The only one who persevered was my nephew, but he didn't live close by. We would drive the kids up to Maine once a year to stay with my nephew for a week. But there were still 51 lonely weeks in a year where these kids were largely invisible.

Kristy went back to work even before the funeral. I don't think she could bring herself to grieve. She threw herself into work and somewhat detached herself, even from the kids. She loved her children and was a great mom when Sam was alive. But something just shattered in her. So, at a very young age, these two kids were left on their own a lot. They did not get directed to a grieving group or get counseling for their loss. So, they began to act out in risky ways. As other men came into their mother's life, it did not go well with them, especially with no psychological help.

Sammy worried about so many things. His school had a "Dunkin' Donuts with Dad" event, and he was in turmoil about what to do. He ended up just staying home. When it was Blair's turn for the event, Sammy did not want her to miss out as he had. He found a hat, used an eyebrow pencil, drew a mustache on his face, and stepped in as 'dad' for her. Such a heavy weight on an 8-year-old. Kristy moved her research to gene testing for disease predisposition. Maybe that was her way to grieve and heal—finding a way to prevent others from the pain and loss she had suffered.

I finally realized why I cried for so long, for so many years. I had to slowly watch the disintegration of this wonderful family and of the life that could have been. It just kills me that I didn't get to watch Sam be the dad he wanted to be, to shepherd them till they were grown. By the time Sammy was 6, Steve had already taken him on so many guy trips. They hiked and camped. Sam loved the New England Patriots and took the kids to games. He loved being a dad, loved every minute of it. When people would say, "Well, Sam's in a better place, I'd say, "BS. He should be here with those kids."

I have all these pictures. I'd planned to make memory books for his kids, but I just couldn't make myself do it. The reminder of what was lost and what could have been was just so heartbreaking. As the kids grew, they became very troublesome to the point that our other kids did not want Sammy and Blair around their own children. Understandable, yet another abandonment. We tried for sleepovers with us as often as we could.

Our faith was another issue. It didn't waver, but my faith was wounded. We had left the Catholic Church during the abuse scandal. Having been abused in my past, I could not stay in a church where that was not only practiced but covered up. Through the suggestion of a friend, we ended up in another church and were immediately directed to join a small group. And I'm here to tell you, if not for the small groups from that church, I don't know where we'd be today. My faith was true, but there was so much pain. The small group took us in and allowed us to cry and mourn without limit. I cried all the time. I could not stop crying, not at church, not at home, not in small group.

Small groups are critical. They're the fellowship God knows we need to survive this fallen world. We were just wrapped in their love for us. They prayed at every juncture, and we could feel it buoy us up. We prayed and prayed. We joined another small group, and both groups never stopped praying for us and our two grandkids. But there's still sadness, and that sadness will never completely go away.

Within my tenuous faith, I still knew God was working on my grandkids. And, finally, a couple months ago—a breakthrough. Sammy, now 15, called and asked to see us again on a regular basis. I was elated but didn't want to push. We suggested coming to take him out to dinner every other week. He countered with 'No, *every* week'. And so, we began. Blair, now 13, still makes excuses to be absent much of the time. She is very troubled, but we continue to reach out to her. She still writes in her dad's legacy book online, and that's something. Her brother is longing for any connection he can have with his family, so there's hope Blair will catch his fervor.

Prayer works.

> I tell Sammy, "You are my goal to live. My purpose is to make sure you know how much your dad loved you and know what kind of a man he was, so you will grow up to emulate him. I'm just not going to go till that's assured in you."

A belief in God is absolutely critical during such passages of life. Joy is a constant in the life of a believer because joy is not happiness. It is the knowledge of God's existence in those who believe in His son and the security of an eternal home with him. God always has a reason and a plan; he's in control. That doesn't mean it's easy. That's why our small groups and the family of God have been so essential.

But happiness returns as well. Spending this time sharing my life story about Sam has been a great revelation and a very healing one for me. Having been able to pinpoint the reasons why my paralyzing grief went on so long—the absence of a great father to two beloved young children—was a game-changer. I purposely press for more expanded family gatherings for these two forlorn grandchildren. I can smile now when I see glimpses of my son in these two precious faces. I can even share a smile and a laugh when I run into folks with such nice things to say about my Sam, even after so much time since his passing. I also delight in making scrapbooks for Blair and Sammy. I'd always planned on doing it but never could. I hope that after presenting them, these beloved grandchildren will know how much they are loved by their family, their father, and their heavenly Father.

It is still hard. Just plain hard sometimes. I miss my son. I miss him all the time. I will always miss him.

Angie

I am Angie, a believer in Jesus, a child of God. Wife to my childhood sweetheart for 33 years, who is now Pastor Jeff of our Assembly of God church. I'm a mother to Rachel, Nicole, Ryan, Nicholas, and one in heaven lost to a miscarriage. Grandmother for three years to Rachel's daughter, Abbie. Secretary and worship leader at our church for many years.

A year ago, we weren't quite empty nesters with Nicholas, 17, still at home. Ryan was 22 and off the reservation, dabbling in the college party life. Nicole was married and settled with her husband, very much in love. Our oldest, Rachel, was 30, married to Fabio with her toddler, Abbie. Our family had its flaws, but whose doesn't? We loved them all, and we loved our church family to pieces. Waking hours were full, rich—blessed. Life was wonderful...till it wasn't.

My son-in-law Fabio is a youth pastor and, after a year of pandemic and lockdown, was finally cleared to go to summer youth camp. So, my daughter Rachel and her 3 yr. old Abbie got to go with me to visit my mom for her birthday. It was a wonderful time of family bonding that we didn't get enough of due to ministry commitments. We got lots of 'girlfriend time' doing fun family visits by day and watching "Laverne and Shirley" together by night. These were rare and precious days, so we treasured every minute.

When we returned home, Fabio presented cold symptoms and got tested for Covid. He was instantly positive, and Rachel freaked out, getting us all tested as well. She was positive, and so was Abbie. I tested negative, so I was tasked with food deliveries to family and friends suffering from the great plague of our time. But within a couple of days, I also started to feel bad and tested positive. This was the wave of the Delta variant.

It felt like a horrible cold that took forever to pass until excruciating nausea and fatigue set in. We called Rachel and her family regularly, even Face Timed. Everything seemed okay. But a little over a week into it, Fabio was having trouble breathing, and Rachel called 911. Fabio was kept in the hospital for nine days, getting oxygen and breathing treatments—the full cocktail. He was discharged on supplemental oxygen, still very weak. Since Abbie was already with me, Fabio came to stay as well.

By now, my whole family had Covid, and 1/3 of our church had it. The next time Rachel called to check in, my mother's intuition felt something wasn't right, so I told her I was coming over with Happy Meals from McDonald's. When I got there, Rachel was not breathing normally. She was breathing from the lower portion of her abdomen, and I knew she had pneumonia. We tested her with her home Oximeter, and her O2 saturation was in the 80's. Anything below 90 means you need help. We drove her to our home, and my husband tested her with our newer Oximeter.

He didn't report the reading, just said, "Take her to the ER, *NOW.*"

Since we were in Covid times, no one could go to the hospital with Rachel. We just had to drop her off. I told her to tell them immediately that she couldn't breathe so she would get seen quickly. She did get seen but was shuttled to a room alone—left for 24 hrs.—with no medical treatment, just the non-stop beeping of machines that no one attended. We would FaceTime or text to check on her. She finally got the whole cocktail, and we started to feel more confident about the attention given to her.

But she later texted me, "I'm not getting better. What if I don't get better? Mommy, can you promise me I won't go on a ventilator?"

I told her I couldn't promise her that, but I could promise that
she was going to be okay. She had been there several days, and
on the afternoon of the 4th day, she called...

"Pray. They're about to intubate me."

I was stunned. I wanted to know why. Someone took the phone
and told me that everything was moving too quickly. The nurse
said that Rachel had a collapsed lung and a pulmonary
embolism. She had no co-morbidities. She'd had a very mild
form of Ataxic Cerebral Palsy as an infant, but it was no longer
an issue.

That was the last time I heard Rachel's voice. I had to call Fabio,
Rachel's husband, who was still hospitalized in another part of
the county. He was shocked and left in disbelief as he struggled
with his own medical crisis. Rachel would be on a ventilator for
31 days, and it was the beginning of a month-long battle with
the hospital to get known protocols to help her heal. We fought
to 'prone' her—flip her face down to ease her breathing. They
refused because they said they were overworked. I would NOT
accept that. These are the times they earn their pay, and you
don't get to kill people because you're tired. Sorry if that seems
harsh, but that's how I felt. This was a blow on the downward
slide.

We also wanted to get Rachel approved for ECMO –
Extracorporeal Membrane Oxygenation—which was not
provided at this hospital. Like dialysis is for the kidneys, ECMO is
for the lungs and heart. She would have to be flown to the
University of Miami in Gainesville. We knew a medical pilot and
had money provided to pay the bill. But the CMO of the hospital
would not sign off and release Rachel, stating she wasn't sick
enough for ECMO. Another low blow, as a friend of the family
had recently gotten off a ventilator and recovered from Covid
with ECMO treatment.

As her mother, I was able to check in on her vitals, and when her
blood pressure dropped, I pushed again for 'proning'. They

refused sighting staff fatigue again, so I approached the
pulmonologist. He would not prone her either, but they did try
to remove the tube each day. When they did, her body would
overreact, and they'd have to give her a sedative and leave the
tube in. I told them she needed to hear us, hear our voices so
her body would remain calm, and maybe they could get the
tube out. We kept fighting and got her a tracheostomy to make
it easier for her to breathe, hoping that would help in removing
the tube.

I often wondered if Rachel being a mouth-breather was an
issue. Her childhood case of Ataxic Cerebral Palsy had left her
that way, and she couldn't do sports like swimming which
required nose-breathing. I wondered if the cannula the hospital
stuck in Rachel's nose giving her oxygen was ineffective because
she wasn't breathing through it. All hindsight now. Another
'what if?'

Being denied closeness from the family in these desperate times
was the hardest part for a struggling patient. I was scrambling
for information and inundated with many well-meaning people
suggesting what course of action to take. I felt helpless, as
though my daughter was being held prisoner inside the hospital
with only the 'current protocol' to treat her. I pushed the
hospital to break protocol and let me stand by the ICU door and
see Rachel in person. They relented, but it was hard. She had
tubes coming from both lungs, tubes everywhere. Fabio tried
but got kicked out. Watching his beloved suffer and struggle
alone was such a helpless feeling for him. It was an answer to
prayer when they agreed to let me see Rachel several times,
though only through the glass. It was hard for me too, but I kept
my cool. This was my baby girl.

Several times hospital staff placed a phone by Rachel's head or
propped up an iPad. Family could talk to her and pray for her via
Zoom, even though she was on paralytics and completely
knocked out—unable to respond to us.

Abbie sang the ABC song. When that didn't work, she sang, "Wake up, Mommy. Wake up, Mommy."

On Aug. 18th, they were saying Rachel's vitals—blood pressure and kidneys—were good, so we assumed she was improving. As I led 'Praise and Worship' that night at church, I had a split-second vision of a white casket in front of me. I thought it was Satan messing with our positive news, and I rebuked him. But in hindsight, I think the Lord was trying to prepare me.

On Aug. 19th, we got a call from the hospital asking if we all wanted to come down and say our 'goodbyes', and now would be a good time to do it. WHAT???!!!! She was improving yesterday!!

We quickly called everyone we could as my husband and I, along with our 17 yr. old son Nicholas rushed to the hospital. Our daughter Nicole and her husband Alex raced from the other side of the city. This time we were somberly ushered in by hospital staff, but they would only allow us to see her one at a time. Nicholas was the first to make it to the ICU. As soon as he saw Rachel, he began crying.

The nurse embraced him, telling him, "It's ok, honey."

But that 17 yr. old son of mine had made friends in high places. He found the CEO of the hospital and gained permission for all of us to go into Rachel together. The last to arrive was our collegiate son Ryan. His hospital ID sticker read that he came in at 5:33 pm. Everyone else had said their goodbyes and retreated to the lobby with our Presbyter and another minister friend. I felt a pressing urge to go with Ryan up to Rachel's room. Once we came to her room, he struck up a career conversation with the nurses, and I remember getting so mad, telling him...

"These are precious moments with your sister that you'll never get back. Career networking doesn't matter. It can come later. Look at her!"

The nurse then entered the room, and as she stood behind Rachel's bed, she said,

"Rachel, your mom, and your other brother are here to visit you."

And as soon as she finished speaking, we watched Rachel's telemetry—her vitals—all plummet downward simultaneously. The nurse made a rude motion, slashing her finger across her throat, and I lost it. I was raised not to say, 'Oh my God', but I couldn't stop myself. I put my hand over my mouth, trying to muffle it, but my spirit was crying out. Oh my God. Oh my God. Oh my God. This was not like TV and movies. My son wrapped his arm around me, pushing me into his side. Rachel's heart stopped at 5:48 pm, just 15 minutes after Ryan arrived.

Fabio had signed a DNR earlier, so there was no rush of hospital activity. The nurse made a little heart sign with her hands and left. We discovered later that shortly before Rachel died, the hospital CMO approved her for ECMO and signed the release. You can imagine how we felt about our healthcare experience.

Now we were faced with the reality of death. As Assembly of God parishioners and Pastors, we believed in the power of the Holy Spirit. We believed in God's healing powers. We'd laid hands on many people and had seen them miraculously healed. And yet God did not heal our Rachel. I had a t-shirt I wore regularly that said, "Faith Not Fear." When I got home, I wadded it up and tossed it.

My sister-in-law, Chessie, had had an urging from the Holy Spirit to come to us even before we knew Rachel was dying, and she made it there the day Rachel passed. She was phenomenal in receiving gifts, organizing tasks, and lightening our load. I knew I would see Rachel's body at the memorial service, but I wanted to prepare myself and see her before then. I asked my sister-in-law and best friend to go with Fabio and me to the funeral home to see her. I wanted the shock taken away, and I wanted to make sure that Rachel looked the way I wanted her to like Rachel.

This was the worst. Let's be honest—nobody looks good dead. And this was my firstborn, my baby girl. The family spent a lot of money on a nice dress, but the mortuary didn't have it sitting right on her. As I adjusted it, I saw where the makeup ended and how purple her skin was. It was shocking. I also noticed her panties showing because they hadn't pulled the dress lining fully down to her knees with the dress. As I went to adjust this and lifted her legs, I suddenly realized her legs were wrapped in plastic. Another jolt. I have no idea why the plastic was, but I assumed it was to contain embalming fluids. When I went to fix her lipstick, I noticed cotton up her nose and wanted to remove it, but I realized it was probably there for the same reason as the plastic around her legs. I wasn't thinking things through, just reacting like a mom, wanting my girl to look her best. What else could I do to care for her anymore? Rachel was gone from me.

They asked me if I wanted some of her hair. I was a zombie but accepted. I went from fighting to keep my daughter alive to the brisk rush to get her body in the ground. Funeral home, caskets, venue, service, slideshow, food, all in such a short time. Thank God for Ativan, which allowed me to function. The medication does not take away your pain but allows you to deal with it in slow motion. It enabled me to get through the tasks and events needed to bring a fitting end to Rachel's time on earth.

We were advised to have Rachel's service at another church so that, when we returned to ministry at our own church, we wouldn't have memories or visualize the casket in our place of worship. It was also anticipated that more mourners would show up for Rachel's 'Celebration of Life' service than our church could hold. This was a wise choice. The service was live-streamed with over 500 attendees and viewed 9,600 times. This fulfilled Rachel's vision of her testimony reaching thousands of people. I used to tell her that she didn't need to have a big platform to have a big message. She would get so mad at me because she truly saw her testimony reaching thousands of people. I should have known better.

The family received those coming to the service, entering a sanctuary bathed in sunflowers. Rachel loved that flower, so sunflowers were placed all around her—placed everywhere. As mourners arrived, they could pick up a small sunflower as a memory, yet most laid their sunflowers in the casket with Rachel. I stood up front with my hand on Rachel's forehead or on her hand because I knew that was the last time I would be able to touch her on earth.

We were inundated with help afterward. There were so many women in my kitchen competing to do the best cooking and cleanup. It was so pragmatic and kind, but eventually, we needed to thank them and send them home. The family needed to face their grief in private.

My husband and I were leaders of a church and barely had two weeks to get back to ministry. We had been present while Rachel was still in the hospital, but everyone was skittish around us now. We assumed that a realization had hit—If the pastor and his family could get serious cases of Covid resulting in death—that it could happen to them too. No one was immune. Rachel had died from Covid along with Oscar, our beloved adult Sunday School teacher who passed just the night before our daughter.

Two weeks was not enough time. As a praise and worship leader, I was too weak. I couldn't get the air up to project my voice into the song. Someone had to lead for me. People were very nice, but no one knew what to say or what not to say. Of course, we heard, 'She's in Heaven,' or my favorite, 'She's in a better place.' Really? She's in the dirt, buried 6ft under! I know they meant well. There's not much you can say. Some people we'd been really close to actually ghosted us. We gave them the benefit of the doubt, understanding that maybe they just didn't know how to deal with us, with the death and the loss. I don't know. Maybe it was fear, the thought it could easily happen to them, and they couldn't let their mind dwell there.

The roughest torment that comes after the crowd dissipates are the questions, the 'what ifs?' What if I hadn't taken her to the ER? What if I'd gotten an attorney to fight for her care? What if we'd yanked her from that hospital and flown her to get ECMO? What if we'd been able to stay close to her, talking and soothing her in her hospital room? What if all the Covid protocols hadn't delayed or prevented some of her potential treatment? Did we do enough to fight for them?

I can point to one dark moment for sure. I went to Rachel's gravesite, which was under a tree. Right there, near her grave, was a package. We had received a lot of gifts, so this wasn't surprising. But I opened it up, only to be horrified by a dead chicken. It was a Santeria sacrifice, a cleansing sacrifice. It's a popular practice here in South Florida, but it was extremely offensive and desecrating to my girl, who truly loved the Lord and His word. I was already angry, and this didn't help.

I wasn't angry with God, just angry at circumstances. But I was confused by God. I had seen people restored to health. I had personally laid my hands on people and seen them healed on the spot. At one point, I had pleaded with the CMO to let me be in the room with Rachel. I'd been with her when she took her first breath, and I demanded to be with her when she took her last. They gave me 10 minutes. I told the nurse I was going to anoint her with oil and pray for her to be healed, so if she didn't want to get in trouble for allowing that, she should turn around. She pulled the curtain and let me be with her for 20 minutes. I anointed Rachel with oil and commanded her to be healed in the name of Jesus. I commanded the illness to leave her body. I did everything I knew to do that had worked in the healing of others in the past. To no avail. I sang "You are My Sunshine" to her along with her favorite worship song, "Here in Your Presence." Even in the funeral home, I prayed for Rachel to 'rise up'.

"In the name of Jesus, rise up!" But she didn't.

I'm still not mad at God. I think I struggle knowing I don't have the control that I thought I had. My thoughts toward healing are different now. We had always believed in the laying on of hands and in God's miraculous healing. We had always understood God was doing the healing and not us. But I think we were just a little bit cocky because we had seen divine healing happen so often. Rachel wasn't physically healed on earth but in heaven. The earthly healing came in us. Our faith level has gone from 'God's going to do it' to 'I trust you'. It's God's choice as to where and how He heals and where and how He shows his glory.

My husband has dealt with his own anger. He gets frustrated when other pastors advertise healing services in very cliché terms. He also rejects referrals for counseling.

"Unless that counselor had a 30 yr. old daughter who died of Covid, they have nothing to offer me."

Together we decided to do something considered a bit rogue in our denomination. We got symbolic tattoos over our hearts: mine—a sunflower, Jeff's—Rachel's portrait. We did them together, side by side. Despite our artwork being mostly hidden due to location, a peek was seen through light summer clothing. And the comments rolled in. One pastor told us he wouldn't "mark up his body for the dead". Another pastor's wife told me she was confronted about my new addition and the scriptural taboo. I asked her how she responded. She said a tattoo was not something she would do, but this tattoo was between Sister Angie and God. I immediately thought, 'good job'. But she wasn't done. She went on to caution me on how I gave my testimony because I wouldn't want to encourage others to get tattoos. I wanted to reach through that phone and do something very unscriptural.

I don't know which moments were the darkest; sometimes, I think I haven't reached them yet. The actual service and burial went by so fast, and at times, I just wanted it to be over with. I can never tell what will trigger the grief. I'm at a high-functioning level of sadness all the time. But sometimes, I bottom out. Spirit-filled pastors' wives shouldn't think like this. Or that. Last night, some little thing set me off, and I was crying so hard my chest hurt like I was giving myself a heart attack. A heart attack in the worst emotional sense. I remember leaving the graveyard on one of my visits and coming to a stoplight. I watched people rushing around to their next stop, singing, arguing, or just intent on their next destination, not knowing what I was suffering. I wanted to yell...

"Do you know where I was? Do you know my baby girl is buried in the ground back there? Do you know how I feel?" I wanted them to stop and understand this, to know what this feels like.

But Hebrews 13:5 always came through, "I will never leave you or forsake you." So, I never once turned my back on God because I know he never once turned his back on me.

Romans 8:28 promises, "And we know that for those who love God, all things work together for good for those who are called according to his purpose." This was fulfilled in our experience through Rachel's death. First and foremost, her testimony was seen by thousands on YouTube and social media. We received so many gifts and gift cards from friends and strangers from all over. Secondly, our family became closer than we had been in years. Something Rachel had prayed for. And thirdly, Ryan—our wild child and party boy—has left that life behind and is walking with the Lord again. Rachel had been praying for this as well. Ryan has joined a praise and worship team at a church near his college and is now married. PTL. I started a blog called "Breaking Protocol" which I hope to get going when the time is right.

Rachel's husband Fabio and our granddaughter lived with us for seven months afterward. It was with them that I had my first laugh-out-loud moment. I wanted to feel guilty, but we had all suffered the same loss, and we all laughed, so it felt okay; it felt right. He works for our good. I am so blessed to share the responsibility of taking care of Abigail while Fabio works.

We have also experienced the supernatural. While sick, our son Ryan dreamed he had entered heaven and was greeted by a very excited Rachel. She had no symptoms of illness whatsoever and immediately wanted to take her brother to see their grandmother, YaYa, and their sibling. I miscarried before Ryan was born. To his disappointment, Ryan woke up before seeing either. We believe this was not a 'dream', but an actual supernatural experience. Another morning without warning…

> Abbie came bounding out of her bedroom, announcing, "I had a dream of Mommy!" She went on to tell us her Mommy called out, "Abbie!" and hugged her.

Then Abbie went on about her daily routine.

When I returned as a worship leader, I started eliminating songs that were too cliché or replete with hyper-faith. I just couldn't sing that. There was one song we were learning before we all got sick with Covid —" Too Good to Not Believe." My first reaction after Rachel's death was 'no'. It's *too* good to believe. I'm not singing that. But now that I've lived through this year of transformation, I understand more fully.

I am Angie, lover of Jesus, the Child of God in whom I trust. There is no formula to prevent illness or death. Everything in this life is transitory, and He must be enough. And so, I sing.

Too Good to Not Believe (abridged)
By Brandon Lake and Cody Carnes

I've lived stories that have proved Your faithfulness
I've seen miracles my mind can't comprehend
And there is beauty in what I can't understand
Jesus, it's You, Jesus, it's You

I believe
You're the wonder-working God
You're the wonder-working God
All the miracles I've seen
Too good to not believe
Too good to not believe
Too good to not believe, oh-oh

And I can't resurrect a man with my own hands
But just the mention of Your name can raise the dead (yeah)
All the glory to the only One who can
Jesus, it's You, Jesus, it's You (come on)

Oh, I believe
We've seen cancer disappear
We've seen broken bodies healed
Don't you tell me He can't do it
Don't you tell me He can't do it

We've seen real life resurrection
We've seen mental health restored
Don't you tell me He can't do it
Don't you tell me He can't do it

We've seen families reunited
We've seen prodigals return (come home)
We've seen troubled souls delivered
We've seen addicts finally freed (finally freed)

We'll see cities in revival
Salvation flood the streets (come on)
Don't you tell me He can't do it
Don't you tell me He can't do it

We'll see glory fill the nations
Like the world has never seen
Don't you tell me He can't do it
'Cause I know that He can

Yes, I believe (I believe)
And You heal because You love
Oh, the miracles we'll see
You're too good to not believe
Too good to not believe (oh, oh-oh-oh-oh)
Too good to not believe

Oh, never stop believing (oh, yes, I believe)
We've seen so much (yes, I believe)
You're the same yesterday, today and forever (too good to not believe)
You can do anything Jesus, You can do anything (I believe, I believe, yeah)
Hallelujah, wonder-working God
Wonder-working God
Don't you ever stop believing
'Cause He's so, so good
So, so good

Epilogue

"Grief is a harsh taskmaster. It scars your soul. You may not be happier for it, but if you rise to meet it, you will be better. "—REJ

As you ponder these stories of love and loss, of suffering and hope, many will still say, "This is not the way it should be. How can I believe in a God that would allow this?"

Understandable. It all feels very unjust. But it is that very sense of justice that proves a just and loving God exists. The God that created you is a God of justice. He created us in His image, and so that sense of justice you feel is implanted in your nature. He is a just and loving God who did not intend for us to live in this damaged world. He created us whole and perfect and placed us in paradise, a place with no sin, sickness, or death. A place we could love and commune in harmony with God our Father directly.

But He also gave us free will because love only comes out of the freedom to choose. And choose we did. We chose the one thing God wanted to protect us from—the knowledge of evil. God acquiesced to our choice, gave us the desire of our arrogant hearts, and removed us from Eden—separating us from communion with Him.

Humanity was left to live with that choice. We struggle to survive in a fallen world that becomes darker and darker, with more disease, more DNA damage, more selfishness, and more evil with each passing generation. You can blame this all on Adam, but we are all sinners who make bad choices. Adam was no different from us. He was just the first to disobey the Father and suffer the consequences of a righteous God. And mankind suffered in his wake, just as future mankind will suffer in the wake of our sin.

But God knew what we would choose, and in His righteous law, there would need to be blood reparation for our sins if we wanted to be in a relationship with Him again. He would offer a way back to Himself. A very costly way, through the life and death of **His** child, **His** only Son.

So, in this damaged world of evil and suffering and child loss, our patient and loving God offered Jesus—His perfect and sinless son—to provide His creation a way back to life and a relationship with Him. He did this once and for all. He did this for you. And if we accept and cover ourselves in Christ's atonement, we will live with Him now to eternity, once again, in that perfect paradise—heaven where there is no sin, sickness, or death. A place where mothers and children are reunited forever, and we will remember our tears no more.

We will hug these beautiful, glorified children and touch their radiant faces for all eternity.

But for now, we must live with the absence of their presence. When love's labor is lost, we must mourn.

Psalm 138:13, 15-16 – *"For you formed my inward parts; you knitted me together in my mother's womb. Your eyes saw my unformed substance; in your book was written the days that were formed for me when as yet there were none."*

Acknowledgment

Anyone involved in this book, in any way, knows there is only one person who deserves special acknowledgment...

1 Timothy 1:27 – "To the King of ages, immortal, invisible, the only God, be honor and glory forever and ever. Amen"

Resources

(This is not an exhaustive list, just sources important to the mommies in this book.)

GriefShare
Address: P.O. Box 1739
Wake Forest, NC 27588-1739
Phone: (800) 395-5755 (US & Canada)
(919) 562-2112 (International)
Email: info@griefshare.org

Umbrella Ministries
Address: 6183 Pasco de Norte
Carlsbad, CA 92011
Phone: (760) 402-4461
Email: helpingmoms@umbrella.ministries.org

Compassionate Friends
Address: 48660 Pontiac Trail #930808
Wixom, MI 48393
Phone: (877) 969-0010
Email: nationaloffice@compassionatefriends.org

Al-Anon
Address: 1600 Corporate Landing Parkway
Virginia Beach, Virginia 23454-5617
Phone: (757) 563-1600
Email: wso@al-anon.org

The Eli Project: Drug and Fentanyl Awareness
Address: 221 Main Street #343
Seal Beach, CA 90740
Phone: (714) 471-8388
Email: perla@projecteli.info

Books

- *The Grief Recovery Handbook by John W. James*
- *Good Grief: A companion for every loss by Granger E. Westberg*
- *Plan B: What do you do when God doesn't show up the way you thought he would? by Pete Wilson*
- *Forgiven and Set Free by Linda Cochrane*
- *Healing a Father's Heart by Linda Cochrane*
- *Coping With Grief: A Guide for the Bereaved Survivor by Bob Baugher, PhD*
- *Shattered: Surviving the Loss of a Child by Gary Roe*

www.ingramcontent.com/pod-product-compliance
Lightning Source LLC
Chambersburg PA
CBHW040757150726
48196CB00009B/601